When Satan Plays Matchmaker

Exploring the Spiritual Side of Narcissism

I0224111

Yashmira Abi

Dedication

First and foremost, this book is dedicated to The Most High Elohim, YAHUAH and His only begotten son. To Him be all the glory.

This book is dedicated to the millions of people who have suffered at the hands of a narcissist. To all those who have struggled to understand and heal from the effects of narcissism, both in themselves and in others, this book is dedicated to you. May its pages bring light, and may its words offer comfort and guidance as you navigate the complex terrain of spiritual warfare and narcissism.

With love and gratitude,

Dr. Yashmira Abi

Preface

No matter what your beliefs are, you cannot deny the existence of the soul. This book will explain the spiritual side of what is behind narcissism. Narcissism has long been recognized as a personality trait characterized by excessive self-love, a sense of entitlement, and a lack of empathy. While many people may display some narcissistic traits, it is important to understand that true narcissism is a deeply ingrained and destructive disorder.

In this book, we will delve into the evil side of narcissism - the part of this disorder that is often overlooked or misunderstood. Narcissism is not simply only about self-absorption and vanity. It is about a complete lack of concern for others, a pathological need for power and control, and an intentional willingness to inflict harm on the people that love them.

It's critical to realize that narcissism affects a wide range of people. It is an issue that has an impact on families, communities, and sometimes even entire countries. I intend to increase awareness of this problem and motivate more people to take action against it by shedding light on the biblical aspects of narcissism.

It is important to note that all subjects regarding spirits or principalities mentioned in this book are for educational purposes only, and not for fascination. So read on, and be prepared to be shocked, saddened, and inspired.

Chapter One: The Realization

You are seated in your living room, your heart pounding as you hear his footsteps moving closer. The husband you once knew has changed into a stranger, a monster that lurks in the shadows and waits to attack. His eyes narrow as he enters the room, signaling that you are in danger. Although you have seen this look before, there is something more sinister about it this time. He stands in your way as you try to back away and find a way out, his face contorted with rage and unadulterated hatred. Your mind falters as you think that this cannot be your husband. Is this really him? Is this the person you fell in love with?

He glares at you with stark, cold eyes that seem to have turned black with wickedness. In that moment, you realize that you are dealing with something much more insidious than just a narcissist. This is evil—pure and simple. You attempt to calm him down by talking to him rationally, but it is futile. He is unlike anything you have ever seen—beyond logic and without empathy.

This book is the story of your journey, and the journey of so many others, as you come face-to-face with the evil side of narcissism. It is a story of survival, perseverance, and the human spirit's ability to overcome even the most difficult challenges. But it is also a story of warning; a reminder that narcissism is not just a harmless personality quirk, but a dangerous and destructive force that can wreak havoc on the lives of those around it. It is a call to action for all of us to recognize the signs of narcissism, and to stand up against it wherever and whenever we encounter it. For the only way we can hope to defeat narcissism is by shining a light on the darkness of its evil side.

By the time you pick up this book, you must have come to the conclusion that you are involved with a narcissist. A sinking feeling of apprehension may come over you as you realize that you are entangled with such a toxic type of person. When you discover that you are dealing with a narcissist, you may experience a range of intense emotions as you realize that you have been abused and manipulated by this person.

At first, you may feel shocked and confused, wondering how you didn't see the signs earlier. You may ask yourself: "How did I let my guard down?" Or you may hear; "I know I am better than this" ringing in your mind. You may also feel a sense of betrayal and disappointment, especially if you trusted the narcissist or had a close relationship with them.

As the reality of the situation sets in, you may begin to feel angry or resentful toward the narcissist. You may feel taken advantage of, manipulated, or abused. You may also find yourself frustrated that you were unable to make the narcissist see things from your perspective or change their behavior. In addition to these negative emotions, you may also feel a sense of grief or loss. You may mourn the relationship you thought you had with the narcissist, and become disappointed about the way things turned out. This grief can be just as intense as mourning the death of a loved one because you are grieving not only the end of the relationship, but also the person you thought the narcissist was and the dreams and hopes you had for your future together.

It is natural to feel sadness, longing, and even despair as you come to terms with the fact that your relationship was not what you thought it was. You may mourn the loss of the love, attention, and validation that you once received from the narcissist. This grief can be complicated by the fact that they may not have been a consistently negative presence in your life. They may have shown glimpses of kindness, humor, and affection that made it difficult to completely let go of the hope that they would change. It is important to give yourself permission to grieve after ending a relationship with a narcissist by allowing yourself to feel the emotions that arise, such as sadness, anger, or confusion.

The truth is that you did nothing wrong except love the wrong person. It is important to remember that narcissists are skilled at manipulating and deceiving others, and it is not your fault that you were taken in by their charm or lies. Narcissists are skilled at presenting a false image of themselves, and people are often drawn to their charm and charisma. Even people with spiritual gifts, such as discernment, have a hard time detecting a narcissist.

According to the Bible, Satan is a master of deception who can transform himself into an angel of light in order to deceive people. 2 Corinthians 11:14 states, "And no wonder, for Satan himself masquerades as an angel of light." (*New International Bible*, 2011/1978, 2 Corinthians 11:14) This verse suggests that Satan can disguise himself as a messenger of God, appearing to be good and righteous while actually being evil and deceptive.

Satan's ability to transform himself is also seen in the story of the temptation of Jesus in the wilderness. In Matthew

4:1-11, Satan appears to Jesus of Nazareth and offers him power and wealth in exchange for his worship. In each of the three temptations, Satan uses scripture to attempt to deceive Jesus, appearing as a wise and knowledgeable teacher. (*New International Bible*, 2011/1978, Matthew 4:1-11) The Bible portrays Satan as a deceptive and manipulative figure who can transform himself in order to deceive people. His ability to disguise himself as an angel of light or a wise teacher makes him a dangerous adversary who can easily lead people astray.

The capacity to present a false self by wearing a mask or persona is a characteristic that Satan shares with narcissists. Just as Satan transformed himself into an "angel of light," so does a narcissist. Narcissists often wear masks or have various personas that hide their true selves from others. The facade that narcissists display to the outside world frequently consists of an idealized version of themselves. They may put significant effort into upholding their image of being self-assured, endearing, and charismatic. Additionally, they might be masters at influencing people and using their charm to dominate those around them.

Narcissists use a mask in a number of ways to manipulate others into acquiescing to what they want. They can turn into just the right person you are looking for in your life. They may also shield their fragile ego from damage and tend to avoid guilt or thoughts of helplessness. By portraying an idealized vision of themselves, they can prevent criticism or rejection. Additionally, the mask helps them maintain their dominance and power over others. It's important to remember that not all narcissists conceal themselves in the same way. Some may be more obvious with their behaviors, while others may be highly skilled at presenting a charismatic version of themselves. Regardless, the angel of light facade cannot last forever. Eventually, Satan reveals himself and his target sees who he truly is behind the mask.

The fact that you fell in love with a narcissist does not make you weak, foolish, or deserving of mistreatment. Narcissists are experts at manipulation, and they use tactics such as love bombing, gaslighting, and triangulation (which I will explain in another chapter) to keep their victims under their control. They also prey on individuals who are kind, empathetic, and nurturing, as these qualities make them more susceptible to manipulation. When you enter into a relationship with a narcissist, you may not realize what you are getting into until it is too late. The narcissist may have been so skilled at hiding their true colors that you were blinded by their masquerade and drawn in by their attention and validation.

It is important to understand that no one is exempt from narcissistic manipulation. Narcissists can be found in all walks of life, and they are skilled at identifying and exploiting vulnerabilities in their victims. Apart from targeting kind, empathetic, and nurturing individuals, they may also target individuals who are going through a difficult time, such as a death in the family or a job loss, as they are more vulnerable to their tactics during times of stress and uncertainty. Falling victim to a narcissist is not a sign of weakness or naivety because anyone can be manipulated by someone who is skilled at preying on their emotions and vulnerabilities.

Chapter Two: The Origin

The word "narcissism" is frequently used in popular culture, but what does it actually mean? It describes a personality disorder that is fundamentally defined by an exaggerated feeling of self-importance, a lack of empathy for others, and a persistent desire for admiration and attention. People who exhibit narcissistic traits consistently find it difficult to build lasting relationships and often feel empty and bored in both their personal and professional lives.

The term narcissism comes from the Greek myth of Narcissus, who was a beautiful young man who became enamored with his own reflection. This story symbolizes the dangers of self-obsession and the negative consequences that can result from an excessive focus on the self. However, I can say with certainty that narcissism is more than just falling in love with one's own reflection.

To understand the origins of narcissism, you have to look back in time, roughly 6000 years ago, when Cain and Able walked the Earth. This could be one of the first displays of narcissistic behavior. The story of Cain and Abel is one of the most well-known stories from the Book of Genesis in the Bible. It tells the story of two brothers, Cain and Abel, and the tragic events that led to the first murder in human history.

Cain and Abel were both farmers who made offerings to God. Abel's offering was accepted by God, while Cain's was not. Genesis 4:2-5 tells how Cain was very angry because of this; "Then the Lord said to Cain, 'Why are you angry? Why is your face downcast? If you do what is right, will you not be accepted? But if you do not do what is right, sin is crouching at your door; it desires to have you, but you must rule over it'" (*New International Bible,* 1982, Genesis 4:6-7).

It is there that God explains that He will accept his offering only if Cain does what is right. However, Cain ignored God's warning and continued to harbor resentment towards Abel. Cain still felt rejected by God even after God told him that if he makes a choice to the right, He will accept him. The text continues with Cain saying to his brother Abel, "Let's go out to the field." While they were in the field, Cain attacked his brother Abel and killed him.

Here we see that Cain's resentment towards his brother influenced him to lure him to the field with the intention to kill him. God confronted Cain about his actions, and Cain responded with a question that has echoed through the ages: "I don't know," he replied. "Am I my brother's keeper?" (*New International Bible,* 1982, Genesis 4:9) The Lord then proceeds to punish Cain by cursing him, and Cain replies to his punishment in verse 13, "Too much to bear."

When we examine this tragedy, we see two brothers; one wounded by rejection to the point where he ignored God's instructions on how he too could be accepted by Him. The reason why Cain's offering was not accepted was because it wasn't his finest. In the Old Testament, offerings had to be to a standard fit for The Most High, and Cain did not give his best offering, yet he still expected God to accept it. Here we see Cain's sense of entitlement.

This is a perfect display of how narcissists expect a reward for doing the bare minimum. We then see how Cain was able to put on the façade as if he just wanted to spend quality time with his brother in the field, but his true intentions were to lure his brother there to murder him. This is an example of the nature of Satan; an "angel of light" with nothing but wicked intentions fueled by jealousy and rage.

When questioned by God, Cain lies and says that he "doesn't know." Then he has the audacity to ask Elohim, creator of all the universe, "Am I my brother's keeper?" Not only did Cain lie, but his words showed that he had no remorse for killing his own brother. Then, when God punishes Cain, he tells Him that his punishment is too much for him to bear; meaning that he cannot take what he just dished out.

Cain's jealousy and anger eventually led him to commit the ultimate act of violence, killing his own brother in a fit of rage. This is a tragic example of how narcissism can lead to destructive behavior and harm to others. Cain displayed narcissistic personality traits that changed his life forever. Here are some common characteristics of individuals with narcissistic traits that people can display in various degrees:

- *Grandiosity*: Individuals with narcissistic traits often have an inflated sense of self-importance and may believe they are superior to others. Notice that Cain had the opportunity to give his best offering but did not. His grandiosity led him to believe that he could just give a subpar offering and the LORD would take it since he is better than others.

- *Need for admiration*: They crave attention, admiration, and validation from others and may go to great lengths to receive it. It could be said that Cain was driven by a desire for God's validation.

● *Lack of empathy*: Individuals with narcissistic traits may have difficulty empathizing with others or understanding their perspectives. After Cain kills Abel, God confronts him and asks where his brother is. Instead of admitting to the murder, Cain responds with a callous and self-centered attitude, saying, "Am I my brother's keeper?" (*New International Bible*, 2011/1978, Genesis 4:9).

● *Sense of entitlement*: They may feel entitled to special treatment, privileges, or resources, and may become angry or resentful when they do not receive them.

● *Arrogance*: They may have a condescending attitude toward others and belittle or demean them.

● *Envy*: They may feel envious of others who they perceive as more successful or talented and may react with hostility or resentment. Cain's jealousy led him to murder instead of trying to please the LORD.

● *Lack of accountability*: They may refuse to take responsibility for their mistakes or failures and blame others or make excuses instead. Notice how Cain never took accountability for his cruel actions against his brother.

- *Low self-esteem*: Despite their outward confidence, individuals with narcissistic traits may have a fragile sense of self-esteem that is easily threatened by criticism and failure.

The severity and extent of these traits can vary greatly, and individuals with narcissistic features may display a combination of these traits. A variety of relationship issues that affect relationships with narcissists can seriously harm a person's emotional health and quality of life. Narcissists frequently rely on their spouses for approval and attention, which can foster a codependent atmosphere in the union. Due to this, it may be challenging for the partner to impose boundaries or end the relationship.

Particularly if they believe their partner is not showing them enough love or appreciation, narcissists may become possessive and jealous of their partner. This can lead to controlling behavior and isolation from friends and family. Narcissistic abuse can also lead to depression, which is characterized by feelings of sadness, hopelessness, and worthlessness. A person may lose interest in activities they once enjoyed, have trouble sleeping, and experience changes in appetite and energy levels.

Narcissistic abuse can cause a person to experience anxiety as well, which is characterized by feelings of worry, fear, and apprehension. Constant anxiety can cause restlessness, insomnia, and bodily manifestations like sweating and heart palpitations. The likelihood of other mental health issues, such as substance abuse, eating disorders, and self-harm can also be raised by narcissistic abuse.

The term narcissism is not explicitly mentioned in the Bible, as the word was not coined until much later. Although the term is not necessarily in the Bible, there are some passages that are often interpreted as cautionary tales against excessive self-love, arrogance, and pride. For example, in the Book of Proverbs, there are several passages that warn against pride and arrogance, such as Proverbs 16:18, which states: "Pride goes before destruction, a haughty spirit before a fall." (*New International Bible*, 2011/1978, Proverbs 16:18) This passage suggests that excessive self-love and pride can lead to downfall.

There are other passages in the Bible that also don't include the term narcissism, but warn against lying and arrogance and promote humility and putting others' needs before one's own. One well-known biblical story that is often interpreted as a cautionary tale against narcissism is that of King Nebuchadnezzar in the Book of Daniel. In this story, King Nebuchadnezzar becomes proud of his wealth and power, and as a result, God punishes him by causing him to lose his sanity and live like an animal. After he humbles himself and acknowledges God's sovereignty, his sanity is restored.

Another example is the Pharisees, who are often cited as an instance of narcissistic behavior. The Pharisees were a group of religious leaders in ancient Israel known for their strict adherence to the law and outward displays of piety. Although they may have had good intentions, Jesus frequently chastised them for their hypocrisy and obsession with status and self-promotion. The Messiah chastises the Pharisees in Matthew 23 by declaring, "They do all their deeds to be seen by others. Because they love the position of honor at feasts, the best seats in synagogues, greetings in public places, and being referred to as a rabbi by others, they make their phylacteries broad and their fringes long" (*English Standard Bible*, n.d., Matthew 23:5-7).

According to this chapter, the Pharisees were less focused on upholding the letter of the law than how they were perceived by others. Instead of the qualities Yahusha Messiah emphasized—humbleness and service—they desired power and prestige.

In Luke 6:6-11, we see another example of a Pharisee questioning Christ's actions and lacking empathy for others. In this passage, Jesus enters the synagogue on the Sabbath day and notices a man with a withered hand. The Pharisees and scribes are watching Jesus closely, hoping to find a reason to accuse Him. The text explains that The Messiah knew their thoughts and asked the man to stand up in front of everyone. He then posed a question to the Pharisees and scribes, "Is it lawful on the Sabbath to do good or to do harm, to save life or to destroy it?" (*New International Bible*, 2011/1978, Luke 6:6-11). Jesus challenged their legalistic interpretation of the Sabbath and highlighted the importance of doing good and showing compassion towards others.

The Pharisees and scribes remained silent, unwilling to answer Jesus' question. Instead, they were filled with anger and frustration that Jesus would heal on the Sabbath day. Their lack of empathy was evident in their refusal to acknowledge the man's suffering and the compassion that Jesus showed him. They are more concerned with their own legalistic interpretation of the law than with the well-being of the man with the withered hand.

Additionally, the Pharisees often demonstrated a lack of empathy and compassion towards those who were marginalized or struggling, which is another characteristic that can be associated with narcissism. Jesus frequently criticized them for their harsh treatment of sinners and narrow-mindedness, calling them "blind guides" and "whitewashed tombs" (*New International Bible,* 2011/1978, Matthew 23:24-27). The Pharisees' lack of empathy towards others was a manifestation of their self-righteousness and legalism. They were more concerned with their own external appearance and adherence to the law than with the needs and struggles of those around them.

In the New Testament, there are also several passages that caution against pride and self-centeredness, such as Philippians 2:3, which states: "Do nothing out of selfish ambition or vain conceit. Rather, in humility value others above yourselves." (*New International Bible*, 2011/1978, Philippians 2:3) This passage encourages believers to prioritize the needs and interests of others over their own desires. These passages can be interpreted as a warning against the destructive consequences of narcissism and a call to prioritize relationships and humility over personal ambition and selfishness.

At its core, narcissism is a manifestation of a deep-seated sense of emptiness and a lack of connection to something greater than oneself. Narcissists often feel disconnected from their own emotions and desires, as well as from the people and experiences around them. They use their focus on the self and their pursuit of admiration and attention to distract themselves from these feelings of emptiness and disconnection.

The spiritual side of narcissism can be understood as a manifestation of a lack of connection to God. In the preface of this book, I mention that no matter what religion you are, you cannot deny the existence of the soul. The soul is a part of your tripartite being, and is the essence of what holds your mind, will, and intellect. The narcissist's soul is free reign for Satan to use to destruct or delay His target from reaching their purpose in life. People who are in the occult admit that when a person is possessed by an unclean spirit, they do not care if they hurt their mother, wife, grandfather, or even their child. Once the demonic forces take over, they execute whatever they are instructed to do.

When it comes to narcissists, they may not be under full demonic possession but rather severe demonic oppression. The difference between the two is that a demonically oppressed person still has control, and their will is not fully taken over by evil. This is why you may have observed that the narcissist you know never had empathy for anything you suffered with. Empathy is the ability to sense or feel another's emotion, and this is what a narcissist lacks.

Notice how they set out to discard you at the most immoral times; such as breaking up with you while you're in the hospital or committing adultery on your birthday. They may start a fight at a wedding or ghost you on your anniversary without a care in the world. They want you to associate memorable events with the pain that they caused. They often have no guilt or remorse for the damage they have done. People who are not narcissists have empathy; that is, they possess the ability to care, they know how mistreatment would make them feel, and they do not need to manipulate people for their own personal gain.

Chapter Three: The Mechanics of the Narcissist

Before we dive deeper into the spiritual aspect of narcissism, let's break down the mechanics of the narcissistic abuse cycle. The narcissistic cycle of abuse is characterized by a pattern of idealizing, devaluing, discarding, and hoovering. During the idealizing phase, a narcissist will make the victim feel special and loved. During the devaluing phase, the narcissist will start to criticize and belittle the victim. In the discarding phase, the narcissist will completely cut off the victim and discard them. Finally, in the hoovering phase, the narcissist will try to reel the victim back in and make them feel loved again. As we move through the phases, we will be able to see how each affects the victim in a more detailed way.

Phase One: Idealize

In the idealizing phase, you are the narcissist's new obsession and they think about you day and night. The narcissist is fascinated by you and may have told you that they have never met anyone like you before. They may swamp you with phone calls to the point where it's overwhelming. The unexpected constant check-ups are not only to keep tabs on you but to establish a dependence upon their presence in your life. When the narcissist stops the "good morning" text that you've gotten so used to, it will leave you wondering why they're acting differently.

In this stage, the love bombing is at an all-time high. Love bombing may appear charming or even innocent, but it is one of the most manipulative tactics that narcissists, and even con artists, use. It consists of intense spats of interest from the narcissist such as constant phone calls, surprise visits, fervent clinginess, or constant compliments. The narcissist may even tell you that they love you very quickly after meeting you or are convinced you two are soul mates. They may become noticeably pushy if they feel you are not reciprocating their efforts. You may feel that something isn't right as they pressure you to make a commitment early in the relationship.

It is in this phase that the narcissist mirrors your personality to get you to think that you two are made for each other. They take on even the smallest traits of your character, such as little phrases that you say. They get you to talk about your goals in life so that they can appear to have those same aspirations. The narcissist bombards you with affection in an effort to make you dependent on the attention high that you get from being around them. The love bombing is so intense that you truly do believe that you have met your soulmate.

What makes love bombing so powerful is that it can make the targeted individual feel like they are the most loved person in the narcissist's world. It has the power to make a person feel cherished and adored by them, but that is all an illusion. This is especially true if the targeted person struggles with low self-esteem. What makes it so addictive is that dopamine levels get a boost when you hear the words "I love you." The feeling of falling in love releases endorphins that really do make you feel euphoric. The goal of the love bombing is to get you addicted to the attention that they give you. Over time, your body starts to crave the dopamine "high" that is released from the love bombing, which leads you to teeter on the edge of obsession over the narcissist. This stage is undoubtedly the most manipulative stage as this type of approach comes from Satan himself.

The beginning of 2 Corinthians 11:3 states, "But I fear, lest by any means, as the serpent beguiled Eve through his subtlety." (*New International Bible*, 2011/1978, 2 Corinthians 11:3) The Bible describes Satan as the most subtle beast in the field. The word "subtle" refers to something that is not immediately obvious or noticeable but rather understated or indirect. In the Book of Genesis, Satan had the ability to charm Eve in a subtle and deceitful fashion by promising her that she would become as God if she ate the fruit that Elohim told her not to eat. Satan's subtlety can also be seen in how he tempts people with worldly pleasures and distractions, making them forget about their spiritual goals and values. He can be very persuasive and often uses half-truths or lies to deceive people.

Satan comes to you as a wolf in sheep's clothing as stated in Matthew 7:15, but in the following verse, we observe that we can recognize these deceitful wolves by the fruit that they offer. (*King James Bible*, 2017/1769, Matthew 7:15) Think about how the narcissist came to you with a smile on their face, bearing gifts and kind words as they hid the true nature of who they really were. Think about how they promised you a healthy marriage, a life filled with riches and international vacations, and all the other empty promises that they made during this time. When you examine the fruit of who these promises are coming from, you quickly see that this person promised you things that they cannot even achieve themselves.

They may have promised you lavish vacations knowing that they are unable to obtain a passport or promised you that they want a healthy marriage with you, but they are already married and have no plans on leaving their partner. This lying devil came to you as an angel of light, giving you hope of a glorious future, only to lead you into his web of deceit. There were absolutely no plans to execute any of what was promised to you, and the truth is that love bombing was simply a tool that set you up to be devalued in the next step within their cycle of narcissistic abuse.

Phase Two: Devalue

The devaluation stage is the second phase of the narcissist abuse cycle. You have settled into a relationship with the narcissist, and they no longer have a need to pull you into the illusion of a wonderful life with them. In this stage of the narcissistic love cycle, the narcissist emotionally tears you down and cripples your sense of self-worth. After building you up in the idealization phase, they now start to attack your self-esteem in the worst way imaginable.

In this phase, they have now come to hate everything they loved in the initial idealization phase. They may have loved how you cooked, but now they eat out before coming home. They may have fawned over how charming you look when you're happy, but now they hate to see you smile.

During this stage, they may start to withhold affection from you and instead bestow it upon others. They may come home late or not come home at all. You may find phone numbers in their pants pockets, or a secret phone in the back of the closet. You may have seen your significant other on a date, but when you confronted them they said that it was impossible for you to have seen them because they were at home sleeping at that time. That was most likely followed up with an "I'm sorry that you thought it was me, but it wasn't."

What they are doing is a brainwashing technique called gaslighting. Gaslighting distorts your own reality and makes you question yourself. Gaslighting can have serious negative effects on the victim's emotional well-being and sense of self. Victims of gaslighting may experience anxiety, depression, self-doubt, and a sense of isolation and loneliness. Narcissists may deny events or conversations that the victim remembers clearly, causing the victim to question their own memory and perception. This can make you second guess yourself and wonder if that really was him in the restaurant having dinner. At this point, they may have even called you insecure or said things like"How dare you not trust me?"; or "After all, we're soulmates, right?"

In the Bible, Satan is often depicted as a master manipulator who uses deception and lies to lead people astray. In this sense, he can be seen as the ultimate gaslighter, using psychological tactics to make people doubt themselves and their faith. One of Satan's most famous manipulations is seen in the story of Adam and Eve in the Bible. Satan convinced Eve to eat the forbidden fruit by creating doubt in her mind and making her question God's motives. In Genesis chapter three, Satan suggests that God is withholding knowledge from Eve, and that she will become like God if she consumes the fruit. After she states that they may eat of every tree except for the tree of life in the garden or they will die, Satan makes Eve second guess what she heard directly from God by telling her that "you will not surely die." This manipulation led to the fall of humanity and the introduction of sin into the world.

Narcissists may blame the victim for things that are not their fault, making the victim feel guilty and responsible for the narcissist's behavior. They may even say it is your fault that they decided to go behind your back and see other people. Narcissists will even go so far as to enlist the help of others to gaslight the victim, such as convincing friends or family members to support their version of events or discredit the victim. They may give contradictory messages or change their story to create confusion and make the victim doubt their own understanding of the situation. No matter what the situation is, you can guarantee that you will be blamed for their unfaithfulness. And if you get upset about their behavior, they will punish you with the silent treatment.

The silent treatment is a manipulation tactic used by narcissists and other toxic people alike. They stop talking to you for hours, days, or even months to punish you when they deem you to be out of hand. This can make you feel confused or hurt by the sudden change in behavior. You may wonder what you did wrong or how to fix the situation. It leaves you bewildered and surprised that a person who was so attached to you before can dissociate from you so quickly. The lack of communication can create a sense of emotional distance and disconnection in the relationship, leaving you feeling rejected, lonely, and isolated. Little do you know, the narcissist is using this tool to manipulate you and conform you into what they want. They know that in turn, the silent treatment will push you to the point where you are the one who reaches out to them.

This is also the stage where the narcissist drastically reduces their affection for you, and it leaves you craving the person you met in the love bomb phase. You notice that you are not getting the same dopamine rush that you experienced before and, like an addict, you find yourself seeking that high again. You start striving to please the narcissist because they have made you believe that you aren't good enough and that's why they aren't treating you as well as they used to. You begin sending more loving text messages to them in hopes of brightening their day and cheering up their seemingly gloomy mood. You start cooking more spectacular dinners, only for them to tell you that they already ate before coming home. You start planning expensive dates in the hope that the narcissist will see your efforts, but you fail to realize that in this phase, there is nothing you can do to please them.

The hard truth is that you will never be treated the same way you were in the love bomb stage. The narcissist starts to show their true colors and you start to sense that something's not right. At first, you may have thought they were just having a bad day. You sympathized with them because you deeply loved the narcissist. After a while, you take their subtle degrading tone personally. Then, subtle insults turn into blatant disrespect. They say you can't do anything right and make fun of your insecurities. As the devaluing stage continues, the name-calling gets more and more intense, to the point where they even defame your character. They may lie about you and tell people that you are crazy. This is especially true when the narcissist slanders your name while showering their new target with fake love.

Once the narcissist senses that you are starting to feel mistreated, they reel you back in with compliments or promises that they know they will never execute. They string you along just enough for you to regain a feeble sense of security in the relationship. They start the devaluing stage because they are ready to move on to the next target with fresh new fuel. But although they have their eyes on a new target, they still need to get as much fuel out of you as they can.

Another reason why the narcissist starts the devaluation phase is because they realize that you require more than what they can give you. You are a person who is capable of sustaining themselves. You are not a dependent person who relies on others for admiration to improve your self-worth. You are an intelligent and strong-willed individual who is also a problem solver. You have a resilience that is unmatchable, and the narcissist knows that. Deep down the narcissist knows that they cannot compare to the strength and poise that you possess. The narcissist has a mindset purely focused on sustaining themselves and makes decisions based on survival rather than love. Relationships with a narcissist will always be one-sided. You know the relationship is unhealthy when nothing that is achieved benefits the both of you, and everything benefits the narcissist.

The devalue stage aims to tear down your self-worth and prepare you for the next phase of the toxic love cycle; the dreaded discard phase.

Phase Three: Discard

During this phase, the narcissistic individual suddenly terminates the relationship with their partner, often with little to no warning, and no regard for the impact this will have on their partner. They may ignore phone calls, texts, and other attempts to contact them, and even block their partner on social media. The narcissistic individual may withdraw all emotional support from their partner, leaving them feeling lonely and isolated. They may stop expressing love, affection, and interest in their partner's life as a way to punish them for not meeting their needs.

The narcissist may place all the blame for the end of the relationship on their partner, claiming that they caused all the problems. They may use this to justify their decision to end the relationship. Usually, the narcissistic individual may have already found a new partner before ending the relationship with their current partner. They may even introduce the new partner to the current partner, as a way of flaunting their new relationship and asserting their power and control.

The reason for the discard can vary, but it often stems from the fact that the narcissistic individual has become bored with the relationship and is no longer getting the admiration and attention they crave. The discard can also occur if the partner has begun questioning the narcissistic individual's behavior. You may have found that after you questioned the narcissist's behavior, they responded as if you made it all up. Not only did they probably call you names such as crazy or bipolar, but they may also have told you that you are just being insecure.

The discard phase can be particularly painful and confusing for the partner, who may have been deeply invested in the relationship. The sudden termination of the relationship can leave the partner feeling rejected, worthless, and traumatized. In many cases, the partner may struggle to understand what went wrong and why the relationship ended so abruptly. The discard phase can also be a trigger for the partner's own healing journey. It can be a time for the partner to reflect on the dynamics of the relationship and to begin the process of reclaiming their self-worth and healing from the psychological wounds inflicted by the narcissistic individual.

Overall, the narcissistic discard phase can be a painful and traumatic experience for the partner. It is important for those who have experienced this phase to recognize that the behavior of the narcissistic individual is not a reflection of their own worth or value as a person.

Phase Four: Ruminate

After the narcissist discards you, you are left with the rumination stage. Rumination is a term that describes the constant thoughts that you are left with when the narcissist discards you. The truth about this phase is that the narcissist abandons you without closure, and they do this on purpose. They know they are leaving you confused as to why they left. They know they are leaving you wondering how a person could abandon you after promising a future together and they know you are questioning why they smeared your name through the mud. All of this leaves you with no closure. If you're waiting for closure from the narcissist, you will be waiting forever.

When it comes to the ruminating phase, you must remember that the narcissist wants total control of your thoughts if they cannot reach your physical body. You may have been the one to discard the narcissist, but you still find it hard to stop thinking about them. In all actuality, you are thinking about the love bombing that first took place in the relationship.

The fantasy that they used to reel you in is the same fantasy that will keep you in a state of rumination after they are gone.

One way to stop this dreadful mind game of overthinking is to stop living in the fantasy of what could have been. Instead, live in the reality of what happened. Write every horrible experience that you have had with them in a list if you must, but you must sever the lies that they promised you. The narcissist had no intention of executing what they promised you in the beginning of the relationship. You have to break free from the lie that was sold to you.

Phase Five: Hoover

The fifth and final cycle of narcissistic abuse is the hoover phase. The "hoover stage" of abuse describes a tactic employed by narcissists to regain control over their victims. This stage is named after the Hoover vacuum cleaner, as the narcissist is essentially trying to suck their victim back into their deceitful web of manipulation.

During this stage, the narcissist may appear regretful, apologetic, and even repentant. They may express their love and affection for you and promise to change their ways. They may stalk your social media accounts on different pages or even ride past your house to keep tabs on what you have been up to. They may supposedly dial your number on accident or text you to see if you're okay. They might reach out from different phone numbers as well. Sometimes they will reach out for what seems like a meaningless conversation.

If you do not respond, they may shower you with affection from a distance by posting pictures of places that you two frequented. Or wearing certain clothes that you may have liked them in, all in the hopes that you pick up on the indirect hoover. They will look for any clue that you are still interested in them. They may also use various manipulation tactics to convince the victim that they are the problem and that they need to change in order to make the relationship work.

The Hoover stage can be a particularly confusing and difficult time for you, as you may wish to believe that the narcissist has truly changed and that the relationship can be salvaged. However, it is important to remember that the Hoover stage is just another form of manipulation and control. The narcissist does not come back into your life because they want a loving, happy relationship with you. Please remember that once the devaluation stage has begun, the relationship will never be the same. The narcissist does not return because they miss you, most of the time, it is because they want to see what they can still get out of you. They miss the attention that they got from you.

Most importantly, even though the narcissist discarded you, they still seek revenge. Yes, you may not have done anything wrong, and you are the victim of abuse in the relationship but in their mind, you are their target for abuse, and how dare you refuse to tolerate it. This stage is particularly challenging because the narcissist may want you to forget about the past, and they may even ask if you two can start fresh. They will also start the love bomb cycle again in hopes of reeling you back into their web. It is important for the victim to recognize this stage for what it is and set clear boundaries to protect themselves from further abuse.

Chapter Four: The Need to Feed

Wealth is treacherous, and the arrogant are never at rest. They open their mouths as wide as the grave, and like death, they are never satisfied. In their greed they have gathered up many nations and swallowed many peoples. –Habakkuk 2:5

In the spirit realm, demonic forces are constantly at work destroying people's lives from behind the scenes, as it were. The doorway that gives these dark forces access is actually your emotions. Negative emotions such as grief, sadness, anger, and jealousy all give the enemy its daily fuel through the narcissist. Therefore, we must be aware of not only what we are feeling, but why we are feeling these emotions. Have you ever suddenly fallen into a bad mood out of nowhere? There would be no logical reasoning for it, but for some reason, you just started feeling angry. Or maybe a flashback from something traumatic that happened to you randomly appears in your mind. You haven't thought of little Sally in twenty years, but suddenly you get a vision of her bullying you in elementary school.

The narcissist has an insatiable appetite for fuel. When the word "fuel" is used in relation to a narcissist, be aware that it refers to the material things or emotional energy the narcissist gets out of its supply. Like cars, narcissists need fuel to drive. Demons that already carry negative energy cannot function without chaos and disorder. The function of a demon is to torment you and delay your divine purpose in life.

You may have noticed that the narcissist starts the most arguments when everything is peaceful. Peace agitates them tremendously. They do not like to get bored, and when all is quiet, they like to start an altercation. The demonic realm requires negative energy constantly, and it needs fuel drawn from your reaction to their negativity. This is why the narcissist will often provoke you to anger without a just cause for an argument. They may cause discord by doing something that they know will agitate you. When a narcissist provokes you, they are often trying to elicit a reaction or response that will feed their need for attention, control, or power. They may intentionally say or do things that are hurtful, insulting, or manipulative to get a rise out of you.

Narcissists thrive on attention and validation, even if it is negative. If you react to their provocation, they see it as a sign that they have power over you and continue to provoke you in the future. If you respond to a narcissist's provocation with anger or aggression, it can escalate the situation and lead to a bigger conflict. This can be dangerous if the narcissist is prone to physical or verbal abuse. If you don't react to a narcissist's provocation, they may use it as an opportunity to make you feel guilty or responsible for their behavior by claiming that you don't care about them. But if you do respond, they may tell you that you are overreacting or being too sensitive, or that you are the one causing the problem.

It is important to remember that you are not responsible for a narcissist's behavior or emotions. You cannot control how they behave or what they say, but you can control your own reactions and responses. If a narcissist provokes you, it's imperative to take a step back, take a deep breath, and respond calmly and assertively. Setting boundaries and limiting contact with the narcissist can also reduce their ability to provoke you.

Narcissists enjoy causing their victims pain and want to see you suffer. Some of them will even go so far as to make sure that you know they are cheating and lying. Not only do they leave clues that they are cheating to hurt you, but to also let you know where you two stand in the relationship. You see, you aren't as important as you thought you were to the narcissist. They also love to gloat about their new target just to smear it in your face and make you wonder why you were not good enough.

This is because their goal is to cause pain in your life. They want to make you second-guess yourself, but most importantly, they want you to feel just as horrible as they do. Every day, narcissists are tormented by the negative thoughts that they wrestle with in their heads. The narcissist is relentless in their pursuit of making you feel worthless, and they will not rest unless they have said or done something that they know will anger you. "For evil people can't sleep until they've done their evil deed for the day. They can't rest until they've caused someone to stumble." (*Bible Hub*, 2004,Proverbs 4:16)

The narcissist is susceptible to demonic influences, and dark forces use the narcissist to do their will. The narcissist is an open vessel or host for demonic playgrounds in this physical realm. They are more open to demonic suggestions and temptations than the average person. Therefore, they are used by the enemy to not only hurt but also tear down the other party. This is also why narcissists commit egregious acts including stealing or adultery with no regard for anyone except themselves.

I remember seeing a couple who were the epitome of marriage. They had it all; the two lovely children, the two-car garage, and the gorgeous family home. This is what today's society calls "goals". Well, it wasn't long into their marriage that the wife started having an affair with the maintenance worker. Now, have you ever wondered why you can see two people in a happy and healthy marriage suddenly have an affair with someone who was the less-than-promising? I even know of a couple who seemingly had it all; both were lawyers, and they did really well together financially. However, it wasn't long before the husband not only had an affair but also conceived a child out of wedlock.

Since narcissists are open vessels that are essential for the enemy, they are constantly used for destruction. In many cases, successful marriages have spouses who suddenly lust after the maintenance man or a high school graduate. This is because of the spirit that convinces their ego that what they have is not enough. Remember narcissists have a big ego, and they are always seeking fuel. This same drive pushes them to always search for new victims to manipulate. They are forever on the hunt for new victims, and they will never be faithful to one person. The narcissist does not appreciate the good people in their life as they are never truly satisfied with what they have.

Chapter Five: A Cursed Thing Will Curse You

Marriage should be honored by all, and the marriage bed kept pure, for God will judge the adulterer and all the sexually immoral. –Hebrews 13:4

Marriage is not only a spiritual union between two people who commit to sharing their lives together, but also a sacred biblical institution as well. Marriage is often referred to as a covenant relationship, as it is an agreement between two people to love, honor, and commit to one another. Marriage is a fundamental part of God's plan for humanity and is used throughout the Bible as an example of God's love for His people.

The Bible speaks highly of marriage and its importance in God's plan. In the Book of Genesis, God creates man and woman and tells them to be fruitful and multiply (Genesis 1:28). The Bible describes the union of Adam and Eve as one of perfect unity. Adam declared that Eve was "bone of my bones, and flesh of my flesh," and the two were naked and unashamed. God gave them the Garden of Eden to live in and all the animals to care for. This clearly establishes the importance of marriage and family in God's plan. Marriage is described in the Bible as a partnership between a man and a woman, with the goal of creating a home and raising children. In the New Testament, Jesus of Nazareth speaks of marriage as a union between one man and one woman. He also speaks of marriage as a lifetime commitment, and that a man should leave his father and mother to be joined to his wife (*New International Bible*, 2011/1978, Matthew 19:5-6).

Marriage is a complex concept, and its goals can vary depending on the people involved. Generally speaking, most people get married for the purpose of creating a lifelong intimate relationship with their partner based on love, commitment, and mutual support. Marriage is a journey of two individuals who come together with the intention of creating a lasting bond and a life together. In a traditional sense, the goal of marriage is to create a secure, loving environment in which a couple can raise children and build a life together. It is a legally recognized union between two people, and it is intended to serve as a foundation for a couple's future generations. Marriage is a public declaration of love, commitment, and dedication, and it is a way to express a couple's devotion to each other. In addition to providing a strong foundation for a relationship, marriage also provides certain legal, financial, and emotional benefits. It is an important milestone in a couple's life, and a commitment intended to last a lifetime.

The Bible is filled with examples of people who made poor choices when it came to marriage. These stories offer valuable lessons about the consequences of marrying the wrong person and the importance of seeking God's guidance in our relationships. One of the most well-known stories about marrying the wrong person is that of Samson and Delilah. In Judges 16, we read how Samson, a judge of Israel, fell in love with a woman named Delilah, who was not a follower of God.

Despite warnings from his own parents and the dangers of getting involved with someone who did not share his faith,

Samson pursued a relationship with Delilah. Ultimately, she betrayed him by cutting his hair, which was the source of his strength, and turning him over to the Philistines. This story illustrates the danger of getting involved with someone who does not share your faith and values, and the consequences of ignoring warnings from those who care about you.

Another example of marrying the wrong person is that of King Ahab and Jezebel. In 1 Kings 16, we read how Ahab, an Israelite king who ruled over the northern kingdom of Israel in the 9th century BCE, married a Phoenician princess named Jezebel who worshiped the false god Baal. Ahab's marriage to Jezebel led to his involvement in her idolatrous practices and the promotion of Baal worship in Israel.

This was a direct violation of the Israelite faith, which recognized Yahuah Elohim as the only true God. Jezebel's influence over Ahab was so great that he became a weak and indecisive ruler who was easily manipulated by his wife and the prophets of Baal. This eventually led to conflict with the prophet Elijah, who challenged the prophets of Baal to a contest on Mount Carmel to determine which God was truly powerful.

Genesis 29 tells the story of Jacob and his two wives, Leah and Rachel. Jacob had intended to marry Rachel, but her father Laban tricked him into marrying Leah first. Jacob was then forced to work for Laban for seven more years in order to marry Rachel as well. This story illustrates the danger of making impulsive decisions and the consequences of not seeking God's guidance in our relationships.

We also have the story of Solomon, who had hundreds of wives and concubines. In 1 Kings 11, we read how these marriages led Solomon astray and caused him to worship false gods. This story illustrates the danger of putting our desires and impulses above God's will and the consequences of not remaining faithful to Him. The Bible offers numerous examples of marrying the wrong person and the consequences that follow. These stories serve as a warning to us to seek God's guidance in our relationships and to choose partners who share our faith and values. By doing so, we can build strong, healthy relationships that honor God and bless our lives.

Those who had to suffer through being married to a narcissist know that it is like being tied to a dark, gloomy cloud that chases away any chance of light in your life. You may have heard the scripture "...Who God puts together let no man put asunder," while you said your vows. Here is the hard truth about that scripture; most marriages are not the will of God. Men can make many plans, but it is the purpose of Elohim that will stand. You may have thought your marriage was of God, but did you consult Him on the matter? Or did you rely on your own free will? It is impossible for God to lie (*Bible Hub,* 2004, Hebrews 6:18), therefore, He will honor your marriage under His permissive will, although that was not His perfect will.

God's permissive will is what He permits through His Word because, as mentioned above, He cannot lie. The permissive will of God is the idea that God allows certain occurrences to take place, even if He does not specifically plan for them. This concept is based on the belief that God is all-knowing and all-powerful; He knows all that is going to happen and has the power to prevent it but chooses to allow it to happen. Since His word says that He honors marriage (*New*

International Bible, 2011/1978, Hebrews 13:4), He will honor it, but that does not mean you are in His perfect will, with the mate that He chose for you before the foundation of the world. "If The Most High Himself put the marriage together, there could be nothing that will put it asunder" (*New International Bible*, 2011/1978, Mark 10:9).

Being married to a narcissist intertwines your soul with theirs. The soul of a narcissist is not only wicked but also used daily by demonic forces in the soul realm. Two souls become one under the covenant of marriage. There have been instances where a person simply enters a relationship and suddenly all hell breaks loose in their lives (pun intended). You may have noticed that while in a relationship with a narcissist, everything seemed to have failed or been drastically negatively affected. The car that you let them drive may have suddenly broken down or the narcissist may have even gotten into an accident while driving it. You yourself may never even have had a car accident. You may suddenly have problems on the job that you have never had before while intertwined with a narcissist.

Their proximity to you is problematic because there will be a time when the narcissist will receive the rotten fruits of their labor, and you do not want to be around when that day comes. I have seen perfectly healthy people lose their minds, homes, and jobs because of their ties to the demons within a narcissist. Scriptures state that the sun shines on the just and the unjust (*YouVersion*, 2023, Matthew 5:45). Just from that scripture alone, we can also reflect on how the narcissist's gray cloud follows not only the narcissist themselves, but the righteous as well.

Chapter Six: Something Old, Something New

A narcissist's 'new supply' refers to the person or people that a narcissist enters into a relationship with after discarding or losing their previous supply. It is important to note that not all narcissists acquire a fresh supply immediately after their previous relationship ends, and not all narcissists engage in romantic relationships. In the majority of cases, the narcissist already has a new interest waiting on the sidelines while they are in a relationship with you.

When a narcissist enters a new relationship, it's often because they need a source of validation, admiration, and attention. The new victim becomes the narcissist's main source of attention, validation, and admiration, which are all essential for their sense of self-worth. The narcissist's new supply is usually targeted because they possess qualities that the narcissist admires or wishes they had. This could be anything from intelligence, beauty, status, or even simply availability.

At the beginning of the relationship, the narcissist will often be charming, affectionate, and attentive to their newly acquired target. They may even appear to be the perfect partner, showering their new victim with love and affection. However, this is all part of the narcissist's manipulation tactics to hook the new supply in and make them dependent on them for validation and attention.

As the relationship progresses, the narcissist's true nature begins to emerge. They may become controlling, manipulative, and emotionally abusive towards their new supply. The narcissist will demand constant attention and admiration and become angry or hostile if their supply fails to meet their expectations. Over time, the new supply will endure the abuse you endured, and often even worse because the narcissist's rath of not being able to torture you is now directed at them.

The way the narcissist controls and manipulates someone new so quickly is through their spell. When you hear the word 'spell', most people think of a person in a pointy witch's hat stirring up a brew over a huge cauldron, but that is not typically the case. This spell is the delusion that the narcissist puts them under that allows them to accept mediocre treatment. Essentially, all a spell is a sequence of words, deeds, or both that are thought to have magical power or effect on particular things, people, or circumstances in the world of magic and sorcery.

Spells can differ significantly depending on the practitioner, the precise components, incantations, and rituals connected with them. While some spells may only rely on the power of spoken or written words, others may call for the use of specific herbs, crystals, or other tangible objects. A spell's intended outcome might also differ greatly, from luring in love or prosperity to shielding oneself from harm or cursing an adversary. Spells are frequently employed in mystical or spiritual practices to bring about a desired result or transformation.

In order for the narcissist to successfully manipulate someone, the target must be under their sedation. The way that the narcissist does this is through the first phase of the narcissistic love cycle. Faking the future in the beginning of the relationship gave way for the narcissistic spell to be crafted. It was during that time that the target constantly visualized the perfect life that they so desperately desired. They fantasized about the narcissist for the majority of the day, and may have even continued to obsess over them in their dreams.

The narcissist then has the ability to capture the thoughts of someone's mind to the point where they may have found it difficult to not think about the narcissist. This mind influence subdues their own thoughts and gives leeway for the narcissist to take more control by replacing thoughts that the person would have had with thoughts of the narcissist. Through this fantasy of the life they want, the new target is now under the narcissist's spell where they will accept the narcissist no matter what the situation may be. This is why the narcissist's new love interest usually knows about you, they may even know that the narcissist is married, or that they have a history of violence, but none of that matters because the new target has fallen in love with the lie of a promising future with the narcissist.

The "new supply" is the narcissist's new partner that they have already started to groom while becoming distant from their other partner during the devaluing phase of the existing relationship. By the time the devaluation stage hits your relationship, the narcissist is already running a smear campaign against you to the new victim. A smear campaign is a deliberate effort to damage someone's reputation or credibility by not only spreading lies; but spreading false, misleading, or negative information about them. The narcissist runs a smear campaign so well that they can influence your closest friends and family. The narcissist's focus for the smear campaign is to paint a picture that you are mentally unstable or even obsessed.

The smear campaign ensures that the new supply thinks you're crazy and unstable. It takes the focus off the terrible events that the narcissist has done to the previous target. It also creates a diversion between the new and old supply because the narcissist knows that if ever there were a chance that the new supply talks to the old supply, their evil would be exposed.

The narcissist love bombs the new supply as they did with you. They also train the new supply to hate you. Their lies make the new supply feel as though their relationship will work, and that they are superior to the old supply. This is all calculated and set up by the narcissist to not only gain the trust of the new supply but also to gain indirect fuel from you. The new supply and the narcissist draw fuel in this way just from thinking that they are hurting you! Their thoughts of you thinking about them feed both of their egos and their need for fuel.

This is exactly why the new supply rubs photos of themselves in a seemingly loving relationship in the old supply's face. Both the narcissist and the new supply hope to trigger jealousy and hurt in you. As a result, the new supply pretends to be happy with the narcissist despite their abuse. The narcissist does not change just because they are with someone else. Soon enough their mask will slip with the new supply just as it did with you. They will be exposed for the horrible person that they are, but the new victim's pride will not let them accept that they made a horrible decision or realize that maybe the old supply wasn't the crazy one after all.

The negative thoughts that both the narcissist and the new victim have about you play like a broken record in their minds. The narcissist is constantly thinking of hurting you, especially when you decide that you are done with them, and the new victim is feeding their own ego by thinking that you are the "crazy ex" that's jealous of their so-called wonderful relationship. They both repeat negative thoughts in their head about you. They visualize hurting you and provoking you to tears. The narcissist chooses someone that is content with carrying on their hurtful intentions toward you. You may be well into your healing journey, you have let things go, and are focusing on yourself now, but this does not mean that the narcissist and their new victim are not still out to target you. The new supplies manufactured hatred for you fuels their negative thoughts. The narcissist despises the fact that you are thriving without them, and they obsess about getting you back into their web of deceit just to wreak havoc again.

Even though the narcissist is with another person, they still ruminate about you—but not because they miss you. The thoughts they have about you are thoughts of relentless revenge and hatred. This correlates with the concept of creating intentions, which is a practice that people of the occult use to cast spells. The idea behind this practice is that thoughts have a powerful energy and can be used to manifest specific desires or outcomes in the physical world. One way that witches and warlocks do this is to repeatedly chant what they set out to do.

Chanting is a common practice in witchcraft that involves repeating a specific set of words or phrases with intention and focus. Chanting can be used for various purposes in witchcraft, such as casting spells or invoking deities. Creating intentions with thoughts is said to be a powerful practice in witchcraft that can be used to manifest specific desires and outcomes as well. Their narcissistic repetitive thoughts and chants are just the same as what the occult practices in their spells. Although the narcissist or their new supply may not be in the occult per se, it does not change the core essence of what they are doing. Their repeated negative thoughts and words about you are another way to open a spiritual door to harm you. This is why it is essential to pray the whole armor God stated in Ephesians 6 over you daily.

Remember this is a spiritual attack and Satan uses people who he knows will develop hatred towards you. The Bible states that hatred for another person is just like murder (*Bible Hub*, 2004, John 3:15). As soon as the new victim joins forces with the narcissist in hating you, you now have two people who are both being used by Satan to throw spiritual darts of destruction into your life. The power of agreement is a pivotal practice in the scriptures and is a remarkable force that can shape our lives, relationships, and even the world around us. When people come together to agree on a common goal or a shared vision, incredible things can happen.

One of the most well-known examples is found in the New Testament in Matthew 18:19-20, where Jesus of Nazareth declares, "Again, truly I tell you that if two of you on earth agree about anything they ask for, it will be done for them by my Father in heaven. For where two or three gather in my name, there am I with them." (*New International Bible*, 2011/ 1978, Matthew 18:19-20) Another example of the power of agreement is found in the Book of Acts. Acts 2:42-47 states that the believers were "together and had everything in common." They were of one mind and heart, and because of their agreement, "the Lord added to their number daily those who were being saved." (*New International Bible*, 2011/1978, Acts 2:42-47) Now just as those are examples where the power of agreement was used within the kingdom of righteousness, Satan also uses this principle to achieve his goals as well.

The story of the Tower of Babel in the Bible is another well-known example of the power of agreement, but in this case, it led to negative consequences. According to Genesis 11:6, God said the people "are one" because they came together on one accord to build the tower; and the LORD said, "Indeed the people are one and they all have one language, and this is what they begin to do; now nothing that they propose to do will be withheld from them." (Genesis 11:6)

At the time, the people of the world spoke one language and agreed to build a tower that would reach the heavens, with the goal of making a name for themselves. Their collective agreement and ambition led to the construction of a city and a tower of impressive height, but their pride and disobedience to God caused Him to intervene. In Genesis 11:7-9, God says, "Come, let us go down and confuse their language so they will not understand each other." (*New International Bible*, 2011/ 1978, Genesis 11:7-9) As a result, the people were unable to understand each other, and the construction of the tower ceased. This story of the Tower of Babel reminds us that the principle of agreement is not just for the kingdom of light, and that we must not be naïve to the strategies of the kingdom of darkness.

The new suppply is obsessed with you because of the lies told to them by the narcissist in the smear campaign. While the narcissist gains fuel from you in the form of attention or resources, the new victim also gains fuel from you; but not in the way most people think. This type of fuel comes in the form of thoughts that I like to call "negative thought attacks". The new victim believed the outlandish lies about you, and now they feel that they have to protect the narcissist at any cost. You may have noticed that the new victim is the narcissists number one advocate. The new supply also believes that you are intensely jealous of them, and this is where the obsession with you begins. They may start to search online for personal information about you, as well as stalk your social media pages. They may make fake profiles, and fantasize about harming you. All along, they are envisioning a competition with you that you know nothing about.

The thought attacks and negative missiles launched at you may be so severe that they can affect your sleep as well. Remember that although you are physically sleeping, your soul is in an unseen realm. People who are suffering from narcissistic abuse often have dreams of the narcissist that haunts them in the physical world. In these dreams, the narcissist could be harming them, or it may not necessarily even be a bad dream, but they will be present. The spirits behind the narcissist (which I will touch on in another chapter) are relentless in their pursuit of you. In addition to praying over your entire armor daily, you must also pray over your dream realm and ethereal state.

It is never a good idea to try and warn the new victim of the narcissist's evil doings. It will only solidify what the narcissist has already said about you in the smear campaign, even though what you are saying may be the truth. Cutting off the narcissist and their new victim by any means necessary is the best course of action. Remember that this person wants to see you suffer just as badly as the narcissist. Block both parties from your phone or social media accounts because the fake happiness posts run rampant if they think you are watching. Once you eliminate yourself from their sight, the game is not as fun for them anymore.

The new victim is under a heavy narcissistic spell, and don't forget that the narcissist purposely chose a person that would be jealous of you. The narcissist has convinced the new victim that you are not only crazy, but also envious of him or her. The new supply may be the total opposite of you, but they are convinced by the narcissist that you are the jealous one. The narcissist does this to boost the low confidence of the new victim to ensure they have access to the fuel that they produce.

This is the reason why narcissists seem to downgrade after you. They choose a new victim that they know will be vulnerable enough to believe the lies they are about to let loose. The narcissist chooses someone with less spark, zeal, and confidence than you to believe their lies. Essentially, the fresh victim turns into the narcissist's minion that aids in hurting you. The supply truly believes that you are just bitter, and they take pride in having the approval of a love-bombing demon manifestation by their side.

Chapter Seven: The Evil Spirits Within Narcissists

As stated previously, the narcissist is the perfect host for demonic influences. The narcissist may not be demonically possessed to the point where the spirit takes over the entire will of a person, but is still under demonic oppression. Meaning the narcissist still has the choice to do right. Please note that just because the narcissist is a host for demonic activity, it does not mean that they do not have control over what they are doing.

For example, when Jesus and His disciples arrived on the eastern shore of the Sea of Galilee, they encountered a man possessed by a legion of demons. A legion is known to be at least 6000 beings, and those renegades of evil spirits were inhabiting that man. He lived in the tomb and the demons in him were so powerful that no one could bind him, even with chains. Upon seeing Jesus, the man ran to Him and fell at His feet. We see here that although he had a constant internal battle with a legion of demons, he *still* had the will to get up and be set free. It is important not to make excuses for the abusive behavior that narcissists display, but we can look into some of the demons that reside within narcissists so that we can better understand how they are influenced by them.

Lilith

One of the spirits that the narcissist hosts is the spirit known as "Lilith." Lilith and narcissism may seem like two unrelated topics, but there are some connections between the two. In mythology, Lilith is believed to have been Adam's first wife before Eve. According to some accounts, Lilith was created at the same time as Adam, from the same dust of the Earth, and was meant to be his equal. However, Lilith refused to submit to Adam and left him to live on her own. It's important to note that Lilith is not mentioned in the Bible, and therefore there is no mention of a "spirit of Lilith" in biblical texts. However, in Isiah 34:14 an animal called "screech owl" is mentioned; "The wild beasts of the desert shall also meet with the wild beasts of the island, and the satyr shall cry to his fellow; the screech owl also shall rest there, and find for herself a place of rest."

If you look up the definition of screech owl in the Strongs concordance, you will see the name Lilith given for word 3917 with a definition of female night demon. (*Strong's Concordance*, 2022) Lilith is often associated with a spirit or female demon that represents a particular set of characteristics and behaviors that include soul-thirsty conquests. This spirit has been called a witch, a night monster, and even a vampire. Lilith is actually a type of vampire spirit whose goal is to suck the life out of an individual. This is not to be confused with the typical vampire image you may have seen in movies. This is a spirit sent to drain you emotionally and physically. Vampire spirits can instill within you mental anguish that leaves you questioning your own moral standards.

Narcissists are highly demanding in terms of your time and energy and may expect you to constantly cater to their needs. This can be exhausting and drain you both physically and emotionally. This type of spirit seeks to diminish everything you have, and leave you with nothing at all. When you were with the narcissist you may have noticed that your finances were mysteriously disappearing, or you had expenses come up that you never had before. If you had dreams where you felt paralyzed and could not talk or get up, you might have been involved with this type of spirit that seeks to literally drain you of your life force.

This spirit is sent to not only drain your finances and health but also suck the life out of you in any way possible. Please note that if the devil cannot reach you himself, He sends wicked and toxic people such as a narcissist to bring evil into your life. We must be aware of the wiles of the enemy so that we can know exactly how to protect ourselves against them in prayer.

Leviathan

Another spirit that influences the narcissist is the spirit of Leviathan. In biblical history, Leviathan is a sea monster or dragon mentioned multiple times in the Old Testament. It is first mentioned in the Book of Job, where it is described as a fearsome creature with impenetrable scales and fiery breath (*New International Bible*, 2011/1978, Job 41:1-3):

> Can you draw out Leviathan with a fishhook or press down his tongue with a cord? Can you put a rope in his nose or pierce his jaw with a hook? Will he make many pleas to you? Will he speak to you soft words?

Leviathan is also mentioned in Psalm 104, where it is described as a creature that God created; "Here is the sea, great and wide, which teems with creatures innumerable, living things both small and great. There go the ships, and Leviathan, which you formed to play in it." (*New International Bible*, 2011/1978, Psalm 104:25-26)

In Isaiah 27:1, Leviathan is referred to as "the twisting serpent" and "the fleeing serpent," and is described as a creature that God will defeat in the end times; "In that day the Lord with his hard and great and strong sword will punish Leviathan the fleeing serpent, Leviathan the twisting serpent, and he will slay the dragon that is in the sea." (*The Lord's Vineyard*, n.d., Isaiah 27:1)

Leviathan is also mentioned in the apocryphal Book of Enoch, where it is described as a sea monster that represents chaos and evil. In this text, Leviathan is identified with the serpent from the Garden of Eden and is said to be the leader of the evil spirits that rebelled against God. Leviathan is sometimes depicted as a giant fish or whale and is sometimes associated with the concept of the primordial chaos that existed before creation.

Leviathan is described as a creature that cannot be tamed or controlled by humans, which highlights its dominance and strength. This image can be interpreted as a warning against the human tendency to seek power and control over others, which can lead to prideful behavior and a disregard for others' needs and rights. Leviathan, commonly referred to as "the twisting serpent" has the ability to twist and manipulate words. They may even twist or distort entire conversations, leaving you confused and often fighting to defend yourself. This is extremely prevalent when talking to a narcissist. I have even heard of a person who had to record their conversations with a narcissist because they would contort their words to the point where they weren't sure what they heard or said. Narcissists cause drama and twist conversations to manipulate the narrative.

Some interpreters have connected the image of Leviathan with the idea of pride, arguing that the creature represents the human desire for power and control. Job 41 labels Leviathan as the king of the proud; "He beholds every high thing; He is king over all the children of pride."

According to this view, the sin of pride leads people to act like Leviathan, seeking to dominate others rather than living in harmony with them. In the biblical Book of Proverbs, pride is identified as one of the seven deadly sins, and is associated with arrogance, haughtiness, and a lack of humility. Proverbs 16:18 says, "Pride goes before destruction, a haughty spirit before a fall." (*New International Bible*, 2011/1978, Proverbs 16:18) Pride is a belief that one is superior to others, deserving of special treatment, and entitled to respect and admiration.

Narcissism and pride can manifest in various ways in a person's life. People with narcissistic tendencies may seek constant validation and attention, often at the expense of others' needs and feelings. They may feel entitled to special privileges or recognition and may become angry or defensive when their sense of self-esteem is challenged. The narcissist tends to blame others for their actions because their pride will not let them admit that they were wrong.

Titus

The next spirit that resides in a narcissist is the spirit of Titus. Please note that this is not the same Titus associated with Paul in the Bible. When The Most High gave me this word, I was initially confused. I remember just going about my daily routine when I heard the voice of The LORD say that "a lot of people know about the spirit of Jezebel, but do not know about the spirit of Titus." (*Bible Hub*, 2004, 2 Corinthians 11:3) (Again, the Titus who destroyed the Temple is not the same person as the Titus mentioned in the Bible.) This word that I heard Elohim say led me to research this Titus who I knew nothing about. I found out that Titus Flavius Caesar Vespasianus Augustus, also known as Titus, was a Roman Emperor who ruled from 79 to 81 CE. He is most famously known for his role in the destruction of the Second Temple in Jerusalem, one of the most important religious sites in Judaism.

In 66 CE, a Jewish revolt against Roman rule began in Judea, and the Roman Empire responded with a brutal military campaign. In 70 CE, Titus (who was the commander of the Roman forces in Judea at the time) laid siege to Jerusalem. After a lengthy siege, the Roman forces breached the city walls and entered the city, where they looted and destroyed the Second Temple. The Temple was believed to contain the Ark of the Covenant, the Holy of Holies, and the menorah, among other sacred artifacts. After the Roman army took control of the Temple, they looted its treasures and set it on fire. The flames quickly spread, and the Temple was destroyed. The destruction of the Temple was a devastating event for the Hebrew people, as it was their center of religious life and identity. It is believed that over a million Hebrews were killed during the Roman campaign, and many more were taken captive and sold into slavery.

From the findings of the research I was led to conduct on Titus, I concluded that the spirit of Titus is a destructive and oppressive spirit. This type of spirit destroys everything it can get its hands on. When you think about the narcissists in your life, you may remember how they crushed your self-esteem.

They may even have had a fit of rage and destroyed items in your home. Broken dishes, televisions, and even baby items were not off limits when it came to the narcissist destroying your possessions. In the smear campaign, they ruined your reputation by slandering your name in hopes of changing how people view you. Narcissists destroy relationships with their need for control, lack of empathy, and harmful behaviors. This spirit of Titus was sent to destroy you in every way it possibly can.

Absalom

The spirit of Absalom refers to a spirit of rebellion, pride, and manipulation. This spirit is characterized by a desire for power and influence, even at the expense of others. It is often associated with those who seek to undermine authority, sow the seeds of division, and create chaos. In the Bible, Absalom was known for his charm and ability to win over people's hearts. Absalom was the third son of King David and is prominently featured in the books of 2 Samuel and 1 Kings in the Bible. Absalom was known for his striking good looks and allure. However, he also had a reputation for being arrogant and manipulative. He used his charisma to gain support and eventually declared himself king in rebellion against his father, King David.

In 2 Samuel 15, we see how Absalom would stand at the entrance to the city and greet people, shaking their hands and hugging them. He would ask about their concerns and complaints, showing interest in their lives and problems. He made himself accessible and available to the people, listening to their grievances and offering solutions. This made people feel valued and heard.

Absalom used his position as the king's son to gain favor with the people that served his father, and portrayed himself as someone who could provide better leadership. In 2 Samuel 15:3, Absalom would say to the people who came to him, "Look, your claims are valid and proper, but there is no representative of the king to hear you." (*New International Bible*, 2011/1978, Samuel 15:3) He was essentially telling the people that David was not fulfilling his duties as king, and that he was the only one who could help them.

Absalom was strategic in his actions and one of his biggest characteristics was that he was charismatic yet deceptive. He drew people in by portraying himself as someone who actually cared about the people's concerns. He was good at faking kindness to a society who had plenty of concerns. Absalom was even able to create discord between King David and his most trusted advisor, Ahithophel. Absalom knew that Ahithophel was a powerful influence on his father and that by turning him against David, he could weaken his father's position.

When we deal with the narcissist, we are dealing with a spirit who appears to be helpful and charming, but in reality they are secretly plotting to take over what you have. This type of spirit disguises itself as the hero you need just in time to save the day. They turn people against you by deceiving them into thinking they mean well, but their intentions are not sincere at all.

Jezebel

One of the most well-known spirits associated with narcissism is the spirit of Jezebel. Jezebel is a prominent figure in the Bible, particularly in the Old Testament. As mentioned earlier, she was the wife of King Ahab, who ruled over the northern kingdom of Israel in the 9th century BCE. Jezebel is often portrayed as an influential queen who was also deeply committed to worshiping the god Baal. Baal, a pagan god of the Canaanites, was believed to be a god of fertility, rain, and agriculture. She built a temple to Baal in Samaria and appointed many prophets and priests to spread her faith.

Jezebel's promotion of Baal worship was a direct violation of the Israelite faith, which recognized Yahuah as the only true God. This led to a spiritual crisis in Israel, with many people turning away from the Hebrew faith and following Baal. Jezebel's influence was so extensive that even King Ahab, who was initially an Israelite, became a devoted follower of Baal as well. Jezebel is also known for her persecution of the prophets of Israel. According to the Bible, she ordered the execution of many of these prophets and replaced them with the prophets of Baal. This led to a confrontation between the prophet Elijah and the prophets of Baal on Mount Carmel, which is described in the Book of Kings.

Jezebel is also associated with the story of Naboth's vineyard, which can be found in the Bible, specifically in the First Book of Kings, Chapter 21. According to Biblical history, Naboth owned a vineyard near the palace of King Ahab of Israel. Ahab wanted to buy the vineyard from Naboth, but Naboth refused to sell it because it had been passed down to him from his ancestors and was considered a family inheritance.

Ahab was upset and when he returned to his palace he sulked and refused to eat. His wife, Jezebel, noticed his distress and asked him what was wrong. When he told her about Naboth's refusal to sell the vineyard, Jezebel came up with a deceitful plan. She wrote letters in Ahab's name, sealed them with his seal, and sent them to the elders and nobles of Naboth's city, instructing them to hold a public feast and to seat Naboth in a prominent place. Then, she arranged for two wicked men to sit beside Naboth and falsely accuse him of cursing God and the king. As a result, Naboth was taken outside the city and publicly stoned to death. Jezebel's manipulative and controlling ways led to the gruesome death of an innocent man.

In the Bible, Jezebel is portrayed as a wicked and immoral woman who led Ahab astray and corrupted Israel. Her name has become synonymous with a woman who is manipulative and evil. Some of the behaviors exhibited by Jezebel in the Bible, such as her need for control and power, her manipulation of others, and her disregard for the feelings of those around her, are also consistent with the characteristics of narcissistic personality disorder. The narcissist has a need for control that they begin to exhibit not long after entering your life. You may remember the narcissist constantly calling you to "check on you", but they were really keeping tabs on your whereabouts. You may remember the narcissist telling you the outlandish things their ex did, and then following up by saying, "but, you're not like that."

What they were doing was controlling you by training you how not to behave. In the relationship, the narcissist may have wanted to take over your home or control your finances but disguised it for the good of the relationship. They may even control your relationship with God. Their use of manipulation to achieve their goals is synonymous with how Jezebel bared false witness against Naboth.

The way Jezebel arranged false accusations against Naboth speaks volumes about the nature of her spirit. Many of you reading this right now are facing false accusations raised against you by the narcissist. The narcissist is notorious for fabricating stories to avoid looking like "the bad guy." Just as Jezebel bared false witness against Naboth to get what she wanted, the narcissist lied to you to get what they wanted.

Even at the very beginning, they lied to you in the love bomb phase to entice you into the actual relationship. They lied to you by promising a future they knew they could never achieve. They had no intention of keeping any of their empty promises. You may also have to deal with constant gaslighting or false accusations in the court system by a narcissist. The true nature of the narcissist is rooted in lying, and there is nothing anyone can do to change that.

Jezebel's belief in her own superiority and her willingness to use any means necessary to achieve her goals also demonstrate a lack of empathy and concern for others, which are hallmarks of narcissistic behavior. She let nothing get in her way, and, like the narcissist's of today, the word "no" triggered resentment in her. She was used to getting her way and no one dared to deny her such treatment. Her treatment of the prophets of Elohim, whom she persecuted and killed, also suggests a lack of empathy and a disregard for the value of human life.

Death

For as much then as the children are partakers of flesh and blood, he also himself likewise took part of the same; that through death he might destroy him that had the power of death, that is, the devil –Hebrews 2:14

The chief spirit of narcissism is the spirit of death. From the verse Hebrews 2:14, we see that Satan holds the power of death. (*Bible Hub*, 2004, Hebrews 2:14) The narcissist has a death spirit living inside them that is indifferent to human life. He may use deception, sinful behaviors, sickness, or violence to achieve his goals. This death does not always have to be physical; it could also be death to your finances, mental health, or relationship with God. If Satan cannot physically kill us, he can use physical circumstances and emotional manipulation to try to harm or destroy us. The Bible portrays Satan as an adversary who seeks to steal, kill, and destroy. This phrase comes from 10:10, where Jesus says, "The thief comes only to steal and kill and destroy; I have come that they may have life, and have it to the full." (*New International Bible*, 2011/1978, John 10:10) Satan's ultimate goal is to oppose God and lead people away from God's will and purposes.

The narcissist is attached to a spirit of death that can spread sickness and disease. While not all illnesses are caused by Satan, he can use physical ailments to discourage and weaken people, causing them to lose hope and faith in God. There are many cases where an individual that has no genetic disposition for cancer receives a cancer diagnosis while in a relationship with a narcissist. Commonly, you see people exhibiting a mystery illness as they have exhausted every test known to man, but cannot find the reason why they are sick. Individuals with a mystery illness may experience physical, emotional, and psychological distress as they seek answers and treatment for their condition. They may also become very accident-prone, to the point where they mistakenly fall or trip over things that are not there. These little accidents may even cause them to undergo major surgery.

Satan seeks to destroy people's physical, emotional, and mental well-being. In the Gospels, Satan is depicted as possessing people, causing them to harm themselves and others. He also seeks to afflict people with sickness and disease, as seen in the case of Job. In the Book of Job, Satan is allowed to afflict Job with painful sores from the soles of his feet to the top of his head (*New International Bible*, 2011/1978, Job 2:6-7). This affliction causes Job physical suffering and leads him to wish for death. Note that in Job 2:6, God told Satan that He could not kill Job, so Satan tormented Job to the point that he wished death upon himself instead. Similarly, narcissists can push you past your mental health boundaries or cause you to experience a psychotic episode. They may have robbed you spiritually of your virtues and time with God. You may have been so sorrowful that you wished for death upon yourself just like Job.

The Nephilim

The Nephilim are a mysterious and controversial group of beings mentioned in the Bible. The word "Nephilim" comes from the Hebrew word "nephil," which means "fallen ones" or "giants" (not to be confused with fallen angels). The origin and nature of the Nephilim have been debated by scholars and theologians for centuries, with various theories and interpretations. In the Bible, the Nephilim are first mentioned in Genesis 6:1-4, which describes a time when "the sons of God" came down to Earth and had relations with human women, giving birth to the Nephilim. The text reads:

> When man began to multiply on the face of the land and daughters were born to them, the sons of God saw that the daughters of man were attractive. And they took as their wives any they chose. Then the Lord said, 'My Spirit shall not abide in man forever, for he is flesh: his days shall be 120 years.' The Nephilim were on the Earth in those days, and also afterward, when the sons of God came into the daughters of man and they bore children to them. These were the mighty men who were of old, the men of renown. (*Bible Hub*, 2004, Genesis 6:1-4)

The children that were born were evil hybrid beings who were known to bring destruction. The offspring of fallen ones and human women were described as "renown" because they were well-known in various parts of the land at the time. The scriptures describe how God decided to send a great flood to destroy the Earth because of the wickedness between these fallen ones and man. (*New International Bible*, 2011/1978, Genesis 6:13).

Although the Nephilim were wiped out during the flood, we see the Nephilim are mentioned again in Numbers 13:33, when the Israelite spies report back to Moses about the land of Canaan. They describe the inhabitants of the land as "great and tall" and say, "We seemed like grasshoppers in our own eyes, and we looked the same to them." (*Bible Hub*, 2004, Numbers 13:33) Some interpret this as a reference to the Nephilim, suggesting that they were still present in the land. In theology this is a controversial topic because if the fallen ones were wiped out during the flood, how were they still occupying Earth in the Book of Numbers chapter 13?

The answer lies in the same verse in Genesis 6:4; "The Nephilim were on the Earth in those days—and also afterward—when the sons of God went to the daughters of humans and had children by them." (*Bible Hub*, 2004, Genesis 6:4) Notice that the text reads, 'and also afterward', meaning that not every fallen one was destroyed in the flood. Some were still existing and breeding the hybrid children that Moses saw in the land of Canaan many years after the flood.

Now, you may be wondering where these children of the fallen ones went. I, as well as a slew of other scholars, believe that these offspring hybrids are still on the Earth. Of course, we do not see actual giants these days, rather we must think spiritually in this matter. For example, for the giants to even have intercourse with human women, they had to either do so spiritually or shapeshift to be able to access and mate with them. A physical giant would not have been able to, but it does not negate the fact that these women bore the children of the giants regardless of how they were conceived.

The scriptures never state that these hybrids disappeared. As previously stated, they continued to live after the flood (see verse from the last chapter). While they may not have their physical bodies as they did when they lived on Earth, their spirits remain the same. As you dive into the characteristics of the Nephilim you will see that they were wicked and corrupt by nature.

For instance, in Genesis 6:2 we learn that the giants looked upon the women and not only lusted after them, but took whichever woman they chose against their will and raped them. "That the sons of God saw the daughters of men, that they were beautiful; and they took wives for themselves of all whom they chose." (*Bible Hub*, 2004, Genesis 6:2)

The Bible portrays the Nephilim as being associated with destruction and wickedness, both in the pre-flood world and in the land of Canaan. The Nephilim never had a reputation as outstanding citizens on Earth, helping mankind for their good. No, these hybrids were not only destructive, but villainous. The offspring of the Nephilim are no different from the evil loins they came from. The Bible states that every seed produces after its own kind (*New International Bible*, 2011/1978, Genesis 1:11).

Therefore, we can conclude that the children of the Nephilim exhibit characteristics of their fathers, which include perverted lust, immoral aptitude, lying, manipulation, intimidation, and overall deviousness. Since the Bible never says that these hybrids disappeared, many Bible scholars such as myself, theorize that the hybrids still continue to torment mankind, and you can recognize them by their fruit.

Along with spirits who reside within them, some people have experienced seeing actual demon manifestations in narcissists. "Demonic manifestations" refer to displays of demonic activity or influence, which can include a variety of physical and emotional symptoms. For example, when the narcissist is enraged, their eyes may turn black or another color which is not their normal eye color. They may hiss like a snake or spit at or on you. Many people have also witnessed the narcissist's deep demonic stare where they are fixated on you like an animal stalking its prey. They may also growl or bite while in a narcissistic demonic rage. These demonic manifestations are more common than most people think and are often ignored.

Chapter Eight: Sounds Familiar

The enemy comes in to steal, kill, and destroy (*New International Bible*, 2011/1978, John 10:10). One goal of narcissists is to distract and delay you from the path you are supposed to be on. Time is valuable and we cannot get it back. There is no machine or magic button that we can press to rewind time in order to undo a mistake we made. We are all graciously given the same twelve hours a day and twelve hours a night to live a life that fulfills the ordained destiny we were put on this Earth to do. The hard truth is that precious time is passing you by when you are in a relationship with a narcissist. If Satan cannot physically kill you, he will severely delay you from the blessings God has for you.

While you are in a relationship with a narcissist your time is being stolen from you right in front of your eyes. The constant arguments distract you and delay you from spending time on improving the gifts that were given to you by God. Constantly wondering why this person is being so mean to you robs you from spending time in prayer. Spending money on a narcissistic relationship literally steals money from your pockets that could have been used to help others. The vicious cycle of a narcissist is a plan from Satan to obstruct you from reaching your purpose in life. If you don't put an end to your relationship with a narcissist, then you could waste valuable years of your life dealing with this wicked person who has no good intentions for you.

A relationship with a narcissist will always be one-sided, meaning that you will always put in more effort to make the relationship work than they do. The narcissists charmed you just enough in the love bombing stage to reel you in. They bought out the best in you so that you could continue to carry the relationship for the rest of its tenure, and not question their love for you. One of the narcissist's goals is to swindle as much as possible from you.

This could include anything from big-ticket items like a deed to a house to petty items like spare change around the house. They even feel entitled to belongings that you may have worked hard for even prior to the relationship, such as a business you started from the ground up or a life insurance policy that ensures your children will be well off after your death. You have to understand that the narcissists were only committed to you when it benefited them. True love is patient, understanding, and kind. Real love is not based on the conditions of what a person can do for you. When a narcissist loves you, they love what you can do for them. They love the superficial feelings they get from you. Their love is conditional because they only love on their terms and conditions. This is partly why they discard people who genuinely love them and move on to the next victim so quickly.

The narcissist has many demonic influences at play inside their physical body. These are demonic influences that will be there long after their physical body faces death, but that doesn't mean the spirit dies with them. After physical death, that spirit still walks through dry places looking for rest, as stated in Matthew 12:4. So even after the narcissist is physically dead, the evil spirit attached to them still has the ability to target you through another individual. This is why you seem to "meet" the same person over and over again in different bodies. It is the same evil spirit from before in a different body returning to target you again! In Matthew 12:44-45 we read of such a thing:

> When the unclean spirit has gone out of a person, it passes through waterless places seeking rest, but finds none. Then it says, 'I will return to the house I left.' When it arrives, it finds the house unoccupied, swept clean and put in order. Then it goes and takes with it seven other spirits more wicked than itself, and they go in and live there. And the final condition of that person is worse than the first. (New *King James Bible*, 1982, Matthew 12:44-45) Please note that your body is referred to as a house in various scriptures.

In the majority of cases, the same spirit that is targeting you is a familiar spirit. In the Bible, familiar spirits are mentioned in several passages, including Leviticus 19:31, Leviticus 20:6, and Deuteronomy 18:11.

In Deuteronomy 18:10-12, it is written:

> There shall not be found among you anyone who... practices witchcraft, or a soothsayer, or one who interprets omens, or a sorcerer, or one who conjures spells, or a medium, or a spiritist, or one who calls up the dead. For all who do these things are an abomination to the Lord. (*New International Bible*, 2011/1978, Deuteronomy 18:10-12)

In the Book of 1 Samuel, we see the story of King Saul consulting with a witch at Endor to summon the spirit of the deceased prophet Samuel. The witch is said to have a "familiar spirit" that can communicate with the dead. However, the Bible portrays this as a sinful act and a violation of God's law. Familiar spirits are often associated with divination, witchcraft, and other forms of occult practices.

Familiar spirits are just what the name implies, spirits that are familiar to you and your family lineage. Just as there is a kingdom of light with heavenly angels who guide and protect us, there are also demonic hosts from Satan sent to not only monitor us, but also wreak havoc in our lives. Many people forget that we deal with evil in the spiritual realm as well. Satan is not omnipresent, meaning he cannot be everywhere at the same time as God can. Since he cannot be in more than one place at a time, he uses his agents such as familiar spirits to assist him.

These spirits monitor your every move to cause friction and discord in your life. Familiar spirits are believed to be demonic entities who seek to deceive or harm people. They are known to be in the family lineage for generations as they can be attached to a person through the womb. These spirits are thought to be subordinate to Satan and to assist him in carrying out his evil purposes in the world. It is believed that familiar spirits have access to knowledge and insights that humans don't, hence the reason why Saul sought out the witch of Endor to conjure up the spirit of Samuel. They may also seek to deceive people by leading them away from the truth of God's word and encouraging them to follow false teachings or beliefs.

Familiar spirits play a crucial role in the narcissist's pursuit of you. Since they monitor your life, they know how to tempt you, what your likes and dislikes are, and what you are most likely to agree to. They are also aware of what triggers you to be angry or depressed. These same spirits know what you want in a life partner, so they will strategically send you a person that is similar to the one you have been looking for. Remember that these spirits have literally spied on you your whole life, so they know key moments that you experienced. They know important dates in your life as well as who you were with when those moments took place. So, when you meet a narcissist, you may have been bombarded with a slew of what I call strange coincidences.

For example, the narcissist that you met in California was from your hometown of Georgia, but somehow you never noticed them. Both of your parents may have shared the same or similar maiden name. Your ex-partner has the same initials as your new partner. You may have similarities when it comes to your family dynamic. One or both of your parents may have been affected by alcohol abuse. On the other hand, one or both of your parents may have gone to the same college but never ran across each other. Your parents or siblings may share similar names or interests.

You may even have had dreams of the narcissist before you met them. And upon meeting them, the dreams of you two may have escalated to the point where you become consumed with the thought of them. These coincidences identify themselves when you may think about the narcissist and all of a sudden, they call you on the phone. This psychic interference is not a coincidence; there are demonic forces at play trying to hold you hostage to the demonic influence that has most likely been monitoring your life. The more strange coincidences between you two, the more likely it is that the relationship is sent from Satan.

These familiar spirits will also ensure that family hardships and traumas are passed down to you. How many times have you heard of a situation where a person's mother was an alcoholic and they ended up marrying an alcoholic just like their mother, or something similar? Some people come from a family where every woman has experienced physical abuse in domestic violence situations. They may have seen their dad abuse their mother but still wind up in an abusive relationship themselves. Maybe you have heard of someone who comes from a family where every couple is divorced, and they also end up divorced.

These spirits, as well as other demonic influences, make sure to successfully match you with a person who will ensure that whatever trauma is in your family will continue through you. As a side note, topics such as familiar spirits and demons are actually more common than you think. It is only in our Western culture that topics such as this are taboo. Countries such as Africa and the Caribbean are well-versed in these topics. Often, our cultural differences can hinder the steps we need to take in order to heal.

It is important to realize that you must abandon any emotions that you may still have for the narcissist. You must realize that the relationship you had was nothing more than a demonic supernatural attack, and you were the target. Many people are spiritually targeted for several reasons, whether it be because you have a great calling in your life or simply because of who you are. You are a soul in your body, and the entities of the dark world hate that. Satan is a fallen angel that knows his time, and the time of his demons, is short. Their end is in a lake of fire, and these dark entities know that.

This is why Satan has such a hatred for what God has made and will love for eternity. God loves His creations, and He designed us to not only live life, but live it more abundantly. Satan hates you and will do anything to kill you, but if he can't then he resorts to wreaking havoc in your life. This is another reason why He sends familiar spirits, as well as other demons, to knock you off your course.

However, when you finally realize that you are dealing with a toxic person who brings nothing but grief, sadness, and pain, you slowly lift the spell you were under. When you see that this person is not who they portrayed themselves to be, and is actually the opposite of what you fell in love with, you lift the veil of the delusion that you were clouded by. As soon as you separate your emotions from your thoughts and see the reality of the situation, you can plan a clear exit without looking back. When you finally break free from the narcissist and move on, the spirit that was sent to target you does not just disappear. No, that spirit will still reside in the spiritual realm, but you will no longer be the target. That demonic presence will eventually find a new victim to torment.

This is why I cannot stress the importance of avoiding any type of contact with the narcissist you broke free from enough. Once you resist the devil, he will flee from you (*New International Bible*, 2011/1978, James 4:7), but you have to submit yourself to God first and foremost. It is only then that you will have the power to resist the devil. This is essential because once the spirit flees from you, it will eventually return to test the waters again and try to tempt you again. This is seen in the Book of Luke when The Messiah Himself was tempted by the devil after submitting himself to God on His 40-day fast. "And when the devil had ended all the temptation, he departed from him for a season." (*Bible Hub*, 2004, Luke 4:13)

Notice that the text states that the devil departed Him for 'a season'. This implies that the Devil will leave for a period of time but will return to try and lure you in again. This means that it will only be a matter of time before the narcissist comes back, showering you with praise and flattering you with their words. However, these compliments are insincere and merely a method to gain your trust and affection. The narcissist has an indescribable deep hatred for you, and the next time they come back to tempt you, if you give in, the scriptures state that the condition that you'll be left in will be worse than before (*New International Bible*, 2011/1978, Luke 11:26).

Chapter Nine: Recovery

You must keep in mind that this is a spiritual battle. In the soul realm, time does not function the same way as it does here in the material world. It is only in this physical realm that we observe time by looking at our clocks or counting days on a calendar. Spirits have no concept of time passing because they are not observers of time. That is a reason why the narcissist has no problem hoovering you ten or twenty years later. Some of them may actually reach out to you ten years later as if you just talked to them yesterday. Spiritually, you are still being targeted by Satan, and the narcissist is a tool to get you to take the bait. This stresses the importance of avoiding any contact with the narcissist because the spirits within them do not return because they are genuinely sorry and want a happy relationship with you, no, they come back seeking to devour and destroy you. In Matthew 12:43-45 we read; "When the unclean spirit has gone out of a person, it passes through waterless places seeking rest, but finds none. Then it says, 'I will return to my house from which I came.' And when it comes, it finds the house empty, swept, and put in order. Then it goes and brings with it seven other spirits more evil than itself, and they enter and dwell there, and the last state of that person is worse than the first..." (*New King James Bible*, Matthew 12:43-45)

Once you have been delivered from this toxic waste of a relationship, do not look back on what you seemed to have lost. The Bible speaks about the dangers of returning to the life that you were delivered from. One example of this is Lot's wife, a character mentioned in the Book of Genesis, specifically in the story of the destruction of the cities of Sodom and Gomorrah. According to the Bible, Lot was a righteous man who lived in Sodom with his wife and daughters. The people of Sodom were known for their wickedness and God decided to destroy the city.

However, God had mercy on Lot and his family and sent two angels to rescue them. The angels warned Lot and his family to flee the city and not look behind them. As they were leaving, Lot's wife looked back and was turned into a pillar of salt. Note that looking back involved Lot's wife glancing over her shoulder and seeing the flames destroy the life she had in Sodom. Looking back was a sign of doubt in the power of God, and having sympathy for what was being destroyed by Him. Having pity on the narcissist may bring swift destruction on yourself. Looking back also represented a lack of respect as Lot's wife should have been grateful for her deliverance from the wicked city. It is essential that you do not go back to what you have been graciously set free from.

After experiencing narcissistic abuse, it's natural to feel guarded and distrustful of others. Rebuilding trust takes time and patience. There are an innumerable amount of people who have experienced the same characteristics of this type of abuse. These types of experiences could connect a young woman in Montana with an older gentleman in Spain if they were to both have a conversation about the ordeals they suffered through from dealing with narcissists. The reason for this is because the traits of a narcissist do not change by location.

This is another sign that this subject is a spiritual battle, as spirits have the same characteristics and do not change, even if the actual human may speak a different language or live in another part of the world. They also do not change because of social class. Anyone from doctors to cashiers battle with narcissist abuse, but you have to remember that the common denominator is the narcissists. Narcissists from all social classes across the world have one thing in common they do not know how to love. This is because the Devil does not love, He hates, and there is no love in him. In John 8:44, the Messiah describes Satan as "a murderer from the beginning, not holding to the truth, for there is no truth in him. When he lies, he speaks his native language, for he is a liar and the father of lies." (New International Bible, 2011/1978, John 8:44)

God's love for you is vast and unconditional. He loves you just the way you are, with all your flaws, mistakes, and imperfections. He sees your heart, your struggles, and your pain, and He deeply cares about you. God's love for you is not dependent on your circumstances, achievements, or failures. He loves you simply because you are His creation, and His love is not a conditional love, but an everlasting one that never fades away. God's love is also forgiving. No matter what you may have done, His love for you is big enough to cover any sin or mistake. You will be forgiven and restored to a right relationship with Him when you come to Him with a repentant heart. His love is not judgmental or condemning, but compassionate and merciful. It is a love that surpasses all understanding and is available to you at all times.

A critical first step toward self-improvement and self-awareness is admitting that you disregarded warning flags, even though you didn't do anything wrong other than fall in love with the wrong person. Red flags are warning signs or signals that indicate potential problems or issues in a situation or relationship. When you ignore these red flags, you may find yourself in a difficult or even dangerous situation. Your intuition is one of the most powerful tools you have as a human being. Intuition is often understood as a natural human ability to perceive and understand something without conscious reasoning or logical explanation.

If you have a feeling or intuition that something is not right or that you are being mistreated, it is imperative to listen to and trust your instincts. Ignoring your intuition can make it easier for the narcissist to continue their harmful behavior and can also lead to negative consequences for your mental and emotional well-being. Sometimes, people ignore their intuition because they want to avoid conflict or fear the consequences of speaking out. In other cases, people may feel that they need to please the narcissist or that they are responsible for the narcissist's behavior.

Often, intuition is ignored because we all want to believe that another person has our best interests in mind. We want to believe that the people we meet are generally good people. Sometimes we see the narcissist exactly how we see ourselves; a good-natured person capable of giving unconditional love. We forget that there is indeed evil in this world, and our intuition gives us subtle nudges when harm is near. It is only when we think with our hearts that we disregard these nudges. It can be difficult to acknowledge that you have ignored red flags, especially if you have invested a lot of time or emotion in the situation or relationship. However, recognizing and accepting that you have ignored these warning signs is a crucial part of taking responsibility for what you allowed to take place.

In the love bombing stage, you may have noticed that the narcissist wanted to learn everything about you right away. They wanted to know small bits of information such as your favorite color to large personal information about your finances. This may have seemed harmless at the time because two people do share somewhat personal information when getting to know each other in any normal healthy start to a relationship. But when it comes to a narcissist, the information you tell them at the beginning will be used against you later. When the devalue stage comes forth, you will find that they use your personal information against you as described in Chapter Three.

To avoid this in the future, you must learn to stop oversharing sensitive information about yourself—particularly when you first meet someone. They especially do not need to know your answer to the question: "What's your type?" The narcissist asks that very question just so they can know who to camouflage themselves as. As you reflect on your past relationship, think about how much you shared with the other person. Did they share as much information? Was the information they shared actually true? The problem with oversharing with a toxic individual is that they store information to exploit you with later.

Setting boundaries is crucial when rebuilding relationships after narcissistic abuse. Be clear about your limits and communicate them assertively. Don't be afraid to say no if someone crosses your boundaries. As a matter of fact, one way to recognize a narcissist is to notice their reaction when you tell them "no" in some way, shape, or form. A person who is not a narcissist is understanding and does not overreact if they cannot have something. It is not normal for an adult to handle the word "no" like a toddler who cannot have that lollipop in the checkout line at the supermarket. Narcissists have an extreme sense of entitlement and cannot handle rejection on any level.

You have to remember that narcissist self-esteem is critically low. You can probably recall the horrible abuse you endured during the devaluation stage when the narcissist mask started to slowly slip away. The narcissist called you names that you may still have trouble forgetting to this day. The secret is that those names they called you are actually how they really feel about themselves. The "you will never amount to anything" and the "you're crazy" play out in their heads like a broken record. They know that you are not any of those things, but they want you to believe that you are. Now it's up to you to change the narrative. If you have a flashback of the derogatory words the narcissist spoke over you, replace it with either a positive affirmation, Bible scripture, or motivational quote. Here are three positive Bible scriptures you can use to replace any harmful words the narcissist said to you:

● "I praise you, for I am fearfully and wonderfully made. Wonderful are your works; my soul knows it very well." (*New International Bible*, 2011/1978, Psalm 139:14)

● "For I know the plans I have for you," declares the LORD, "plans to prosper you and not to harm you, plans to give you hope and a future. (*New International Bible*, 2011/1978, Jeremiah 29:11)

- "Why, even the hairs of your head are all numbered. Fear not; you are of more value than many sparrows." (*New International Bible*, 2011/ 1978, Luke 12:7)

At some point in your healing journey, you may feel enraged when reflecting on the mistreatment you have endured. Seeking revenge on a narcissist is a normal and understandable reaction to the pain and trauma of narcissistic abuse. However, it's important to prioritize your own well-being and focus on healing rather than getting caught up in a cycle of anger and resentment. Attempting to get revenge on a narcissist is likely to backfire and only cause more harm to yourself. Narcissists are skilled at manipulating others and may use your actions as justification for even more abusive behavior.

Additionally, revenge often involves stooping to the same level as the person who wronged you, which can erode your own sense of self-worth and integrity. It is often more beneficial to disengage from a narcissist and focus on healing and building a healthier life for yourself. Simply healing and doing well for yourself makes the narcissist sick, so there is no need to retaliate. The narcissist wanted to leave you with your self-worth crushed, and your mental health destroyed. They wanted to financially ruin you as well. They weren't fully satisfied until they saw you hit rock bottom. They hate the thought of you thriving in this world without them; so live your best life! Become the terrific person you were before the abuse or reinvent yourself into a new confident person who is capable of setting boundaries. Do not lose hope; it is never too late to become the person you were destined to be! "For to him that is joined to all the living there is hope: for a living dog is better than a dead lion." (*New International Bible*, 2011/1978, Ecclesiastes 9:4)

It is also important to know that you have to eliminate yourself entirely from this situation. This is because there are times when the narcissist's punishment will not come if you are still in the relationship. In the Book of Genesis chapter 18, Abraham asks God, "What if there are fifty righteous ones in the city? Will You really sweep it away and not spare the place for the sake of the fifty righteous ones who are there? In verse 26, Elohim replies by saying, "If I find fifty righteous people in the city of Sodom, I will spare the whole place for their sake." Abraham continues to ask God if he would still destroy the city if he found thirty, twenty, and then ten righteous people. In verse 32, God patiently replies, "For the sake of ten, I will not destroy it." (*Bible Hub*, 2004, Genesis 18:26)

From those verses, we see that God would have spared the whole wicked city if he had found at least ten righteous people in the land. Just how God would not have destroyed that city if he found any righteous people there, God will spare the punishment of the narcissist if a righteous person is still connected to them. Many times, God is not only storying up the iniquity of the wicked for His day of wrath, but God is also waiting on you to move out of the way of His vengeance. "Do not be deceived, God is not mocked; for whatever a man sows, that he will also reap." (*King James Bible*, 2017/1769, Galatian 6:7)

While it is natural to feel like you would like to get revenge on the narcissist, I can assure you that the narcissist has their day of rectification coming. Throughout scripture Elohim gives

His due justice to the wicked of the land. The Bible talks about God's justice for the wicked in several places. In the Old Testament, the Book of Psalms frequently speaks about the justice of Elohim, including Psalm 37:28, which says, "For the LORD loves justice and will not forsake his faithful ones. The wicked will be completely destroyed; the offspring of the righteous will inherit the land." (*New International Bible*, 2011/1978, Psalm 37:28) In the Book of Proverbs, it says, "The Lord detests the way of the wicked but he loves those who pursue righteousness" (*New International Bible*, 2011/1978, Proverbs 15:9).

Similarly, in Isaiah 3:11, it says, "Woe to the wicked! Disaster is upon them! They will be paid back for what their hands have done." (*Bible Hub*, 2004, Isaiah 3) In the New Testament, the apostle Paul talks about God's justice in his letter to the Romans. He says, "Do not take revenge, my dear friends, but leave room for God's wrath, for it is written: 'It is mine to avenge; I will repay,' says the Lord" (*New International Bible*, 2011/1978, Romans 12:19).

These passages and others in the Bible affirm that God is just and will ultimately bring justice to the wicked. However, it's important to note that the Bible also teaches forgiveness and mercy, and that God desires that all people turn away from wickedness and find salvation through His Son Messiah Yahusha. As the Messiah Himself said in Matthew 5:44, "Love your enemies and pray for those who persecute you." (*New International Bible*, 2011/1978, Matthew 5:44).

During the relationship, the narcissist may have people assist them in their evil doings. They may have told friends to lie to you to uphold their image. They may have had friends cover for them while they were off with a new victim. Maybe their family knew about an adulterous affair the narcissist had, but instead of having a heart-to-heart conversation with them, they actually supported the cheating. There may be many circumstances where family and friends condone and defend the narcissist's immoral behavior. Contrary to popular belief, the scriptures tell us that the people who condone evil are just as wicked as the evil-doer. Proverbs 17:15 states, "Acquitting the guilty and condemning the innocent—the LORD detests them both." (*King James Bible*, 2017/1769, Proverbs 17:15)

From that verse you read that Yahuah hates both the evildoer *and* the person who condones the evil. Isaiah 5:20 states, "Woe to those who call evil good and good evil, who turn darkness to light and light to darkness, who replace bitter with sweet and sweet with bitter." (*Bible Hub*, 2004, Isaiah 5:20) The scriptures continue to describe how the wicked and those who support evil will not be spared from the wrath of God. Scripture also states in Proverbs 17:13, "Whoever rewards evil for good, Evil will not depart from his house." (*King James Bible*, 2017/1769, Proverbs 17:13)

The level of revenge that the narcissist is due is too severe for you to handle. The narcissist has traits in them that The Most High absolutely hates, and some of them are even an abomination. Proverbs 6:16-19 states that "There are six things the LORD hates, seven that are detestable to him: haughty eyes, a lying tongue, hands that shed innocent blood, a heart that devises wicked schemes, feet that are quick to rush into evil, a false witness who pours out lies and a person who stirs up conflict in the community." (*New International Bible*, 2011/1978, Proverbs 6:16-19).

Every one of these listed dwells in the narcissist so it is safe to say that The LORD hated the fact that you were lied to. He hated the fact that you were triangulated and the victim of wicked schemes. Proverbs 19:5 declares that "A false witness will not go unpunished, and he who breathes out lies will not escape." (*New International Bible*, 2011/1978, Proverbs 19:5)

Conclusion

On this recovery journey, you've undoubtedly gained the ability to identify the behavioral patterns that held you back in the past by now, and you've decided to take the difficult step of letting them go. Also, you have come to recognize that narcissism's dark and dangerous side is a force that can seriously harm those who are around it. Romans 12:2 states "...but be transformed by the renewing of your mind." (*New International Bible*, 2011/1978, Romans 12:2). The renewal of your mind starts with giving up your own will so that God can transform your mind. Overcoming this type of abuse takes a divine mental transformation.

As you continue to experience spiritual healing because you decided to face the suffering and trauma of your past, recognize that you have come so far on this journey, and you should be proud of yourself. You have mastered the art of accepting and loving yourself exactly as you are, flaws and all. You have experienced a level of contentment and tranquility that you never imagined was possible; it's the kind of peace that transcends all understanding. Self-love repair after narcissistic abuse might be difficult, but it is possible. Be optimistic and hopeful as you look to the future. Understand that there will be ups and downs but know that you are prepared to handle them bravely and gracefully.

With the knowledge that God has given you the capacity to lead the life you deserve, be eager to see what the future holds. A life free from discomfort, anguish, and the restrictions imposed on you by narcissists. Although narcissists are becoming more rampant in society, it is important to not assume that everyone is a narcissist. Rather, know the signs of narcissism and walk in the other direction as soon as you see a red flag. It is possible to form satisfying, helpful connections that improve your well-being and aid in your personal growth. You can establish healthy boundaries and select healthy partners where trust is established gradually.

Most importantly, you cannot be totally healed and set free from this type of vile abuse unless you submit yourself to The Most High. Only He has the power to sever every wicked narcissist relationship. He holds the power to utterly destroy familiar spirits and demons assigned to hinder your progress. The power of God devours the spirit of death as he has given you life, and called you to live life more abundantly (*New International Bible*, 2011/1978, John 10:10).

Many times, God allowed the narcissist to hurt you just enough to get you back to where you needed to be with Him. The narcissist was on assignment to replace the relationship with God in your life. Be somewhat grateful for the narcissists because if it weren't for them, you might not have prayed as you do now. The torment you went through made you dust your Bible off and get back into the word of Elohim. Be thankful that the relationship brought you back on your knees seeking God, because if it hadn't, you would still be under the delusion of the narcissist. If it hadn't been for the heartbreak, you would still be living in the dark of not knowing the seriousness of the abuse you endured.

This is why it is of utmost importance to forgive the narcissist. Someone once said, "People come into your life for a reason, a season, or a lifetime." According to this theory, some relationships are intended to last for a specific amount of time while others might last longer. Even though it might be difficult to let go of the person you thought genuinely loved you, being aware of the idea of a "seasonal" relationship can help you progress on your healing journey.

As you close the book on your narcissistic recovery journey, realize that this is just the beginning. In the future, there will no doubt be more difficulties and obstacles for you to conquer, but now you are confident that you have the fortitude and fortitude to do so. You have learned to appreciate life's joys and rewards by living in the present. Life is a priceless treasure that is frequently ignored. We get a fresh chance to live, love, and change the world every day when we wake up.

However, it is all too simple to lose sight of how fleeting life is and how easily it can be taken away. Close this book with a sense of accomplishment and pride. You have overcome the darkness of narcissism and emerged stronger and wiser on the other side. You are ready to embrace the light and love that life has to offer, and you know that you are worthy of it all. Feel a sense of completion and closure as you finish this book. Know that the knowledge and insight you have gained from this book will stay with you for the rest of your life. You now hold the power and knowledge on how to realign your destiny to God's perfect will. Not only close this book with the assurance that you are more than a conqueror, close this book as a symbol of another chapter of your life... closed.

Prayers

It is important to come to the Father with a heart of repentance; meaning that you acknowledge that you have made a decision to come into a relationship with a narcissist, and now that you see the truth about the situation, you come out of agreement with what Satan had planned for you. Please note that I am accustomed to praying using the Hebrew name of the Messiah who the world calls Jesus of Nazareth. This prayer should be read out loud:

Father, I come to you in the name of Messiah Yahusha, Father I repent of my sin of making the narcissist an idol in my life. I repent for ignoring your word, and I come to you fully submitting myself to your will. Matthew 18:18, states that you have given me the keys to the kingdom and whatsoever I bind on earth will be bound in heaven. Father, in the name of Messiah Yahusha, I bind all familiar spirits and demonic entities on assignment in my life to be chained to the pit and tortured there before their time. I lose the blessings that you have for me as a righteous seed of Abraham. I come out of agreement with the plans Satan had for me, and I ask that every evil covenant established be covered by the blood of Messiah Yahusha. Father, your word declares in Jeremiah 29:11, that you know the plans that you have for me, plans to prosper and not harm. Father, I come into full agreement with the plans you have for me. In Isiah 54:17, Your word declares that no weapon formed against me shall prosper, and I have the power to condemn every evil tongue risen up in judgment against me. Father, right now I condemn every evil word directed at me by the narcissist or anyone else, may those words never come to fruition, and I decree and declare all evil thoughts, plans, and devices of Satan and his agents powerless in my life by the blood of Messiah. Joel 2:25 states that you will restore what the locust has eaten, therefore I stand on your word of restoration. Father, restore unto me the time wasted in the wrong relationship. Redirect me and realign me with the person who you ordained for me. Father I thank you, and decree and declare all retaliations from Satan forbidden. This I declare in the mighty name of Messiah Yahusha.

So be these things.

About the Author

Dr. Yashmira Abi is a multi-talented individual who has pursued a diverse range of academic and professional interests throughout her life. Dr. Abi discovered a deep passion for teaching and advocating for individuals with disabilities, particularly in the area of education law. In addition to her love of special education, she made the decision to enroll in seminary to further explore her faith as well as to gain a deeper understanding of the bible. She completed her studies in 2020 and earned a doctorate degree in Theology. Currently, Dr. Abi is pursuing another doctorate degree in Special Education while actively involved in advocacy work for survivors of abuse including narcissistic abuse. She hosts a podcast focused on bible based spirituality and healing from narcissistic abuse as well as an online ministry. Connect with her on:

Facebook[1]
Narcissism and Spiritual Warfare Youtube[2]
Kingdom Keys Ministry Youtube[3]
Spotify Podcast[4]
Apple Podcast[5]

Thank you for reading
Kindly, Please Leave a Review!
Leave A Review Here[6]

---

1. http://facebook.com/dryayahmarie

2. https://youtube.com/@DrYayahMarie

3. https://youtube.com/@kingdomkeysteaching

4. https://open.spotify.com/show/2aXDGXD8rhNHNXjsUODaxb

5. https://podcasts.apple.com/us/podcast/narcissis-sick-with-dr-yayah-marie/id1677203417

6. https://www.amazon.com/review/create-review/
   edit?ie=UTF8&channel=glance-detail&asin=B0C5JRVNHX

References

1 john 3:15 - love one another. Bible Hub. (2004a). https://biblehub.com/1_john/3-15.htm

2 corinthians 11:3 - paul and the false apostles. Bible Hub. (2011). https://biblehub.com/2_corinthians/11-3.htm

Bible gateway passage: 2 corinthians 11:14 - new international version. Bible Gateway. (2011a). https://www.biblegateway.com/passage/?search=2+Corinthians+11%3A14&version=NIV

Bible gateway passage: 2 samuel 15 - new international version. Bible Gateway. (2011b). https://www.biblegateway.com/passage/?search=2+Samuel+15&version=NIV

Bible gateway passage: Acts 2:42-47 - new international version. Bible Gateway. (2011c). https://www.biblegateway.com/passage/?search=Acts+2%3A42-47&version=NIV

Bible gateway passage: Deuteronomy 18:11-12 - new international version. Bible Gateway. (2011d). https://www.biblegateway.com/passage/?search=Deuteronomy+18%3A11-12&version=NIV

Bible gateway passage: Ecclesiastes 9:4 - new international version. Bible Gateway. (2011e).

https://www.biblegateway.com/passage/?search=Ecclesiastes+9%3A4&version=NIV

Bible gateway passage: Galatians 6:7 - new international version. Galatians 6:7 KJV - - Bible Gateway. (2011). https://www.biblegateway.com/passage/?search=Galatians%2B6%3A7&version=KJV

Bible gateway passage: Genesis 11:7-9 - new international version. Bible Gateway. (2011h). https://www.biblegateway.com/passage/?search=Genesis+11%3A7-9&version=NIV

Bible gateway passage: Genesis 1:11 - new international version. Bible Gateway. (2011f). https://www.biblegateway.com/passage/?search=genesis1%3A11&version=NIV

Bible gateway passage: Genesis 4 - new international version. Genesis 4 NIV - - bible gateway. (2011). https://www.biblegateway.com/passage/?search=Genesis%2B4&version=NIV

Bible gateway passage: Genesis 6:13 - new international version. Bible Gateway. (2011g). https://www.biblegateway.com/passage/?search=Genesis+6%3A13&version=NIV

Bible gateway passage: Hebrews 13:4 - new international version. Hebrews 13:4 NIV - - bible gateway. (2011). https://www.biblegateway.com/passage/?search=hebrews%2B13%3A4&version=NIV

Bible gateway passage: James 4:7 - new international version. Bible Gateway. (2011i). https://www.biblegateway.com/passage/?search=James+4%3A7&version=NIV

Bible gateway passage: Jeremiah 29:11 - new international version. Bible Gateway. (2011j). https://www.biblegateway.com/passage/?search=Jeremiah+29%3A11&version=NIV

Bible gateway passage: Job 2:6-7 - new international version. Bible Gateway. (2011k). https://www.biblegateway.com/passage/?search=Job+2%3A6-7&version=NIV

Bible gateway passage: Job 41:1-3 - new international version. Bible Gateway. (2011l). https://www.biblegateway.com/passage/?search=Job+41%3A1-3&version=NIV

Bible gateway passage: John 10:10 - new international version. Bible Gateway. (2011n). https://www.biblegateway.com/passage/?search=John+10%3A10&version=NIV

Bible gateway passage: John 8:44 - new international version. Bible Gateway. (2011m).

https://www.biblegateway.com/passage/?search=John+8%3A44&version=NIV

Bible gateway passage: Luke 11:26 - new international version. Luke 11:26 NIV - - bible gateway. (2011). https://www.biblegateway.com/passage/?search=Luke%2B11%3A26&version=NIV

Bible gateway passage: Luke 12:7 - new international version. Bible Gateway. (2011p). https://www.biblegateway.com/passage/?search=Luke+12%3A7&version=NIV

Bible gateway passage: Luke 6:6-11 - new international version. Bible Gateway. (2011o). https://www.biblegateway.com/passage/?search=Luke+6%3A6-11&version=NIV

Bible gateway passage: Mark 10:9 - new international version. Bible Gateway. (2011q). https://www.biblegateway.com/passage/?search=Mark+10%3A9&version=NIV

Bible gateway passage: Matthew 12:43-45 - new king James version. Bible Gateway. (1982). https://www.biblegateway.com/passage/?search=Matthew+12%3A43-45&version=NKJV

Bible gateway passage: Matthew 18:19-20 - new international version. Bible Gateway. (2011t).

https://www.biblegateway.com/
passage/?search=Matthew+18%3A19-20&version=NIV

*Bible gateway passage: Matthew 18:19-20 - new
international version*. Bible Gateway. (2011u).
https://www.biblegateway.com/
passage/?search=Matthew+18%3A19-20&version=NIV

*Bible gateway passage: Matthew 19:5-6 - new
international version*. Bible Gateway. (2011v).
https://www.biblegateway.com/
passage/?search=Matthew+19%3A5-6&version=NIV

*Bible gateway passage: Matthew 23:24-27 - new
international version*. Bible Gateway. (2011w).
https://www.biblegateway.com/
passage/?search=Matthew+23%3A24-27&version=NIV

*Bible gateway passage: Matthew 23:5 - new
international version*. Matthew 23:5 ESV - - Bible
Gateway. (2011). https://www.biblegateway.com/
passage/?search=Matthew%2B23%3A5&version=ESV

*Bible gateway passage: Matthew 4:1-11 - new
international version*. Bible Gateway. (2011r).
https://www.biblegateway.com/
passage/?search=Matthew+4%3A1-11&version=NIV

*Bible gateway passage: Matthew 5:44 - new
international version*. Bible Gateway. (2011s).

https://www.biblegateway.com/passage/?search=Matthew+5%3A44&version=NIV

Bible gateway passage: Matthew 7:15 - king James Version. Bible Gateway. (2017a). https://www.biblegateway.com/passage/?search=Matthew+7%3A15&version=KJV

Bible gateway passage: Philippians 2:3 - new international version. Bible Gateway. (2011x). https://www.biblegateway.com/passage/?search=Philippians+2%3A3&version=NIV

Bible gateway passage: Proverbs 15:9 - new international version. Bible Gateway. (2011z). https://www.biblegateway.com/passage/?search=Proverbs+15%3A9&version=NIV

Bible gateway passage: Proverbs 16:18 - new international version. Bible Gateway. (2011aa). https://www.biblegateway.com/passage/?search=Proverbs+16%3A18&version=NIV

Bible gateway passage: Proverbs 17:13 - king james version. Bible Gateway. (2017b). https://www.biblegateway.com/passage/?search=Proverbs+17%3A13&version=KJV

Bible gateway passage: Proverbs 19:15 - new international version. Proverbs 19:5 ESV - - bible gateway. (2011). https://www.biblegateway.com/ passage/?search=Proverbs%2B19%3A5&version=ESV

Bible gateway passage: Proverbs 6:16-19 - new international version. Bible Gateway. (2011y). https://www.biblegateway.com/ passage/?search=Proverbs+6%3A16-19&version=NIV

Bible gateway passage: Psalm 104:25-26 - new international version. Bible Gateway. (2011ab). https://www.biblegateway.com/ passage/?search=Psalm+104%3A25-26&version=NIV

Bible gateway passage: Psalm 139:14 - new international version. Bible Gateway. (2011ac). https://www.biblegateway.com/ passage/?search=Psalm+139%3A14&version=NIV

Bible gateway passage: Psalm 37:28 - new international version. Bible Gateway. (n.d.). https://www.biblegateway.com/ passage/?search=Psalm+37%3A28&version=NIV

Bible gateway passage: Romans 12:19 - new international version. Bible Gateway. (2011ad). https://www.biblegateway.com/ passage/?search=Romans+12%3A19&version=NIV

Bible gateway passage: Romans 12:2 - new international version. Romans 12:2 NIV - - bible gateway. (2011). https://www.biblegateway.com/passage/?search=romans%2B12%3A2&version=NIV

Genesis 18:26 - abraham begs for sodom. Bible Hub. (2004d). https://biblehub.com/genesis/18-26.htm

Genesis 6:2 - corruption on the Earth. Bible Hub. (2004b). https://biblehub.com/genesis/6-2.htm

Genesis 6:4 - corruption on the Earth. Bible Hub. (2004c). https://biblehub.com/genesis/6-4.htm

Hebrews 2:15 - jesus like his brothers. Bible Hub. (2004e). https://biblehub.com/hebrews/2-15.htm

Hebrews 6:18 KJV: That by two immutable things, in which it was impossible for god to lie, we might have a strong consolation, who have fled for refuge to lay hold upon the hope set before us:. Bible Hub. (2004f). https://biblehub.com/kjv/hebrews/6-18.htm

Isaiah 27:1 - the lord's vineyard. Bible Hub. (2004h). https://biblehub.com/isaiah/27-1.htm

Isaiah 3 - judgment on jerusalem and judah. Bible Hub. (2004g). https://biblehub.com/niv/isaiah/3.htm

Luke 4 - the temptation of jesus. Luke 4 KJV. (2004). https://biblehub.com/kjv/luke/4.htm

Matthew 5:45 that ye may be the children of your father which is in heaven: For he maketh his sun to rise on the evil and on the good, and sendeth rain on the just and on the unjust.: King James Version (KJV): Download the bible app now. YouVersion | The Bible App | Bible.com. (2023). https://www.bible.com/bible/1/MAT.5.45.KJV

Numbers 13:33 - the reports of the spies. Bible Hub. (2004i). https://biblehub.com/numbers/13-33.htm

Proverbs 4:16 - a father's instruction. Bible Hub. (2004j). https://biblehub.com/proverbs/4-16.htm

Strong's concordance. Strong's Concordance. (2022). https://strongsconcordance.org/results.html?k=screech%2Bowl